D0915733

THE WORLD OF

Flannery O'Connor

THE WORLD OF

Flannery O'Connor

JOSEPHINE HENDIN

Indiana University Press

BLOOMINGTON / LONDON

036772

Published in Canada by Fitzhenry & Whiteside Limited, Don Mills, Ontario

Library of Congress catalog card number: 76-108208
SBN: 253-19340-0

Manufactured in the United States of America

FOR HERB

CONTENTS

ACKNOWLEDGMENTS

I WOULD LIKE TO THANK Mrs. Regina O'Connor for her kindness in granting me an interview, and for showing me Milledgeville.

I am also very grateful to Mrs. F. H. Harding of the Mary Vinson Memorial Library in Milledgeville for so patiently showing me the O'Connor collection, and to Mrs. Sally Foster of the Milledgeville *Union-Recorder*, who made my research there a pleasure.

I am particularly grateful to Dr. Rosa Lee Walton, former chairman of the English Department of the Georgia College at Milledgeville. My talk with her about O'Connor's fiction was as stimulating as it was pleasurable.

I would like to thank all the people of Milledgeville who were kind enough to share their impressions of Flannery O'Connor with me. Although they preferred to remain anonymous, their contribution to this book is clear.

I would like to thank Dr. and Mrs. Alfred Messer of Atlanta for their hospitality. My conversations with Dr. Messer of Emory University were both illuminating and enjoyable.

My thanks also go to Professor William York Tindall of Columbia University, who first introduced me to Flannery

O'Connor's fiction; to Professor John Unterecker of Columbia University, whose enthusiasm for my work was a great source of encouragement; and to Professor Joseph V. Ridgely of Columbia University, who read my manuscript and made many valuable suggestions for improving it.

Greatest of all is my debt to my husband, Herbert Hendin, whose stimulation, encouragement, and affection made this book possible.

J. H.

New York

September, 1969

Key to references in text to O'Connor's work

E   EVERYTHING THAT RISES MUST CONVERGE

G   A GOOD MAN IS HARD TO FIND

V   THE VIOLENT BEAR IT AWAY

W   WISE BLOOD

THE WORLD OF

Flannery O'Connor

I

In Search of Flannery O'Connor

Flannery O'Connor's world is like the forest of Parzifal with a railroad running through it—a curious mixture of the traditional and the modern. Using conventional themes for new effects, she writes about the collision of the present with the past, reflecting the diversity of life in an art of violent contradictions. Against an optimistic view of life in which man is perfectible by reason and technology, she sets a blacker image of life as unredeemable pain—of man as simply an organism containing juices in irreversible flow. If you listen only slightly you can hear a more contemporary Settembrini and Naphta argue in the Georgia hills, far from the magic mountain, and not in the language of ideas, but in the "good country talk" O'Connor loves so well.

In most discussions of her work, it has been customary to regard O'Connor as a more orthodox Naphta, a spokesman for the Roman Catholic Church, and a writer of fugues on the doctrine of *felix culpa*. Although this has led to a number of insights into her work, I think it has also tended to distort it—to reduce it to a series of illustrations of church dogma. Even though Flannery O'Connor's debt to her church may have been great, it did not leave her a pauper. She was, I think, more artist than preacher. If you listen beyond the "moral debate," if you listen more than slightly, you can hear the voice of Flannery O'Connor, the writer who was much more than a polemicist.

Most critics have not only ignored the voice of the artist, they have refused to see the believer behind the belief. They write about O'Connor's "message" as though her religion had nothing to do with her life. They entirely divorce theology from human experience. Yet the church not only differs in character from country to country (it has become a cliché to cite the differences between Irish and Italian Catholicism, for example), or even from region to region; it may have a distinct personal significance for each of its members. It is a gross oversimplification of faith to assume that religion or art can spring from universal theological abstractions.

The impulse to write or to pray grows from some more complex force, a necessity that must be rooted in the concrete, the particular experience. For Flannery O'Connor, I suspect that necessity had more to do with being Irish-American, a Southern woman, the offspring of an old Georgia family, and a victim of lupus, the wasting, degenerative disease that struck her at twenty-five and eventually killed her, than with being part of the Roman Catholic Church. Nor is it enough merely to say that Flannery O'Connor was an Irish-American Catholic writer who lived in Milledgeville, Georgia, went to Father Toomey's church and to specialists in Atlanta. Disturbing questions will always arise: What did the church mean for Flannery O'Connor? How did she handle her illness? What is the experience of life in a small patrician town that has not forgotten it was the last Confederate capital of Georgia?

What answers you can find are even more disturbing than the questions. For if you go in search of Flannery O'Connor, now five years dead, you will not find an articulate ghost. You will find no less than two Flannery O'Connors: the perfect daughter who lives on in her mother's memory, the uncompromising Catholic O'Connor has become for so many of her readers; and the more enigmatic writer of those strange and violent tales. From the tension between these disparate selves—between O'Connor as Catholic daughter and O'Connor as writer—you begin to get some idea of the complexity of her character, a complexity she concealed so thoroughly that you are almost inclined to think that Flannery O'Connor's greatest and most spontaneous fiction was her life. At any rate, it seems to me that both her peculiar Catholicism and her violent art grew from the contradiction she lived.

When Flannery O'Connor died in 1964, the Milledgeville *Union-Recorder* said the most flattering things. They called her "one of our state's ornaments," a writer famous because of her "spiritual life" whose work "had a rare and exalted quality" which, they add, "was dramatized by the usually humble people whose career illustrated her themes." She had a sensibility so perfectly balanced that she could raise burros, swans, and peacocks, and write, with equal pleasure. To the Milledgeville *Union-Recorder*, Mary Flannery O'Connor (1925-1964) was no less than the daughter of Regina Cline O'Connor, whose family has, for more than one hundred years, been one of the most distinguished in Milledgeville. (Mr. O'Connor was from Savannah.)

The Cline House, where O'Connor spent most of her adolescence, was built around 1820 and was, for a while, the Governor's House. You can see behind the thickly planted dogwood the brick fence built by slaves, surprisingly graceful but bowed out now, uneven and laced with cobwebs. Through the fence you can see Shot, the Negro hand, slowly tending the lush, overgrown garden, looking as though he has been there forever, cutting back the same long vines. White fluted columns rise almost perfectly straight from the oddly tilted front porch. As I came toward the house, Regina O'Connor came out on the porch to show me in.

It is impossible not to be struck by this woman with hard blue eyes. She is indeterminately old and looks deceptively frail among the Cline family portraits that fill her parlors. Infants, girls with sausage curls, and impressively mustachioed men rest everywhere on the highly polished end tables. O'Connor's picture is there too. It has taken its place alongside of generation after generation of Clines who are spoken of as though still alive. Even the furniture seems to have acquired some living, human qualities. Desks, pianos, chairs—each has made its odyssey through life, visited cousins in another town, and come back.

It is impossible not to admire Regina Cline O'Connor's relation to this house, her sense of herself, her allegiance to her family and her immense self-assurance. She quotes her daughter with pride and conviction: " 'If you know who you are, you can go anywhere.' Flannery said that." And indeed she did, but with some misgivings.

Mrs. O'Connor manages her house and her affairs with the assurance of a woman who knows who she is, and still more, what she wants. Beset by pigeons, she imported snakes from an Atlanta five-and-ten to destroy them, filled her birdbath with flowers, and has not been bothered since. At least, not by pigeons. The squirrels have lately begun to eat her dogwood buds.

From the Cline House you can walk through boxwood and lavender bordered gardens to the "new" Governor's Mansion (1838), where Governor Brown and his wife celebrated the secession of Georgia and later "entertained" General Sherman, who marched through Milledgeville in November of 1864 and, as one Milledgeviller has it, poured molasses in the organ of the Presbyterian church. The Mansion has been restored to something of its former self. It is filled with Milledgeville ladies, English Regency furniture, Chippendale pieces, and a couple of Hepplewhite sideboards. Its curator-manager is an old family friend of the O'Connors, a very gracious lady who seems to know the lineage of everyone in the county and of every important armoire. She seems convinced that O'Connor would have been enthusiastic about the restoration had she lived. O'Connor *was* fond of having lunch with her mother at the Sanford House ("a perfect piece of federal period architecture"), which, in the last two years, has been rescued from its site between a Piggly Wiggly supermarket and a Trailways bus terminal. It's now on a tree-lined street, among other white columned homes, where it will become a museum. I began to feel, as the ladies talked, that O'Connor herself, in taking her place alongside of generation after generation of Cline ghosts, has somehow achieved the status of a Hepplewhite chest. She's displayed to advantage, her scars are concealed or acknowledged as a sign of her authenticity, and she is said to contain all of those neatly folded Southern virtues. She revered the traditions of her family, had beautiful manners and an equanimity so stable that, when she was sixteen and her father died, she could comfort her mother by reminding her that he was better off than they were.

But O'Connor left Milledgeville to become a writer "on her own" as Robert Fitzgerald, her friend and literary executor, says in his introduction to *Everything That Rises Must Converge*. After getting her Master of Fine Arts degree in writing from the University of Iowa, she came to New York; not a surprising move for a woman of twenty-three who wants to be anything "on her own." What is surprising is that she so quickly left New York to live on

an isolated Connecticut farm as the boarder of the Fitzgerald family. The "shy, glum girl" Fitzgerald describes
seems to have needed isolation, thrived on friendships
maintained through letters or kept with married friends
over friendly drinks. The only child of a self-consciously
patrician family, praised by her mother for not seeking out
friends but waiting until they came to her, seems never to
have been deeply close to anyone. Even her friendship with
the Fitzgeralds had to be carried on through the mails after
she became ill.

Her life on the Connecticut farm, devoted to days of
writing and evenings of conversation with Sally and Robert Fitzgerald, was the life she chose for herself when still
"on her own." It was not so very different from the life
her illness later imposed on her. Flannery became ill "up
there," said Mrs. O'Connor, referring to Connecticut and
the North in general. She returned to Georgia for a visit
and a check-up. And she stayed.

In the early throes of her disease, O'Connor and her
mother moved from town to their farm, Andalusia, just
outside of Milledgeville. The severe white farmhouse with
its wide, screened porch was O'Connor's home for about
fourteen years. It stands on a hill, its porch overlooking a
wide lawn that slopes into a road. Below the road is a small
valley with a pond. The Negro farm hands live off to the
left in a weathered gray building that looks especially
shabby next to the peacocks O'Connor raised and adored.
A few birds still strut about, oblivious to everything but
themselves. They have long since eaten all of Mrs. O'Connor's flowers and have turned parts of the lawn white with
droppings. They are gorgeous. Beyond the farm hands'
house, there are small hills rolling into the distance.

There is something enormously monotonous and still
about the farm. You can hear the geese bleat from time to

time, or the sharp yowl of the peacocks. Sitting on the porch listening to Mrs. O'Connor's pride in the girl who "did her work" while others "fooled around," listening to her accounts of how happy her daughter was here, entertaining with lively discussions the admiring people who sought her out to talk, the silence seemed to grow. Mrs. O'Connor prefers not to talk about O'Connor's work or her illness. Nor will she permit anyone to see the specialist who treated her daughter. She seems to feel that talking of O'Connor's illness will "prolong" it and prefers to remember the serious, wry girl who has become so famous. Mrs. O'Connor will tell you no more about O'Connor than you will learn from the *Union-Recorder*. In fact, you get the feeling that it was she who, along with a gift of peacock feathers, bestowed on the newspaper her image of a dutiful daughter. And on one level, her image is perfectly true.

Sitting on this porch, I felt for the first time that O'Connor's disease did not radically change her life. Its horror was that it prevented her life from changing at all. The loneliness it dictated for her was all too familiar to the "shy, glum girl" whose feelings had always been so under control, who seemed so essentially alone everywhere. Her illness seems only to have reinforced and cemented an isolation that had always existed, a feeling of being "other" that she could at times accept with wry good humor. I am thinking in particular of a cartoon she did as an undergraduate at the Georgia Women's College. It shows a girl who looks like O'Connor wearing huge eyeglasses and sitting alone at a dance while couples dance all around her. She has a desperately cheerful smile. "Oh well," the caption reads, "I can always be a Ph.D."

If O'Connor joked about what bothered her as an undergraduate, she would later mask a greater pain in frenetic good cheer, treating her weakness and disfigurement humorously and turning herself into a cartoon character. "I am doing fairly well these days, though I am practically baldheaded on top and have a watermelon face," she wrote to the Fitzgeralds at twenty-eight. At thirty-eight, some twelve weeks before her death, she wrote to Richard Stern "a letter scarcely different from any I'd received from her in the five years we'd known each other except that the signature was pencilled and shaky." The letter reads:

> Milledgeville
> [April 14]
> 1964

Dear Richard,

I'm cheered my Chicago agent is keeping up with his duty to keep you informed on my state of being. It ain't much but I'm able to take nourishment and participate in a few . . . rallies. You're that much better off than me, scrapping Tuesday what you wrote Monday. All I've written this year have been a few letters. I have a little contribution to human understanding in the Spring Sewanee but I wrote that last year. You might read something called Gogol's Wife if you haven't already—by one of those Eyetalians, I forget which. As for me I don't read anything but the newspaper and the Bible. Everybody else did that it would be a better world.

Our springs done come and gone. It is summer here. My muscovy duck is setting under the back steps. I have two new swans who sit on the grass and converse with each other in low tones while the peacocks scream and holler. You just ought to leave that place you teach at and come teach in one of our excellent military colleges or female academies where you could get something good to eat. One of these days you will see the light and I'll be the first to shake your hand. . . .

Cheers and thanks for thinking of me. I think of you
often in that cold place among them interleckchuls.

FLANNERY[1]

O'Connor's toughness in the face of her own dissolution
may, as most people say, be admirable and courageous. Yet
it is not enough to say that it is merely this, although it is
less painful to do so. It seems to me to also express her
older, more essential malaise—that deep isolation that seems
to have made her only comfortable when alone in an insulated and protected world, in a world where the most constant and enduring attachment is to swans, ducks, and
peacocks. If it is an affirmation of life at all, it is an affirmation of the life of a very lonely child. Her illness seems to
have made it possible, perhaps essential, that she play this
role for life: the Georgia hick, the farmboy wit who likes
to poke fun at complexity and northern "interleckchuls."
This tough, rather boyish, cheery idiom seems to have been
one of her salvations. It seems to me to be a distinctively
Southern salvation.

What Flannery O'Connor took from her background
was the ability to disappear into her behavior—to become
the role she played to such an extent that she could detach
herself from her own pain. In all her cheerful patter, you
miss entirely the sense of suffering that must have been its
ultimate source. The country diction is oddly mute about
the anguish of a woman feeling the slow violence of disease. It is in fact so inexpressive of anything humanly true
that its silence becomes eloquent. What this silence says no
one can know for sure.

Whatever happened to her or whatever she felt, Flannery O'Connor seems to have followed, quite rigidly, the

code. Not the code of the Catholic Church but the more rigorous code of Southern, genteel womanhood, the code that *forbids* confession. This is the code she would have heard from childhood in those wonderful proverbs: "Pretty is as pretty does," or, more threateningly, "Don't fuss!," or, as Regina Cline O'Connor put it, "I was brought up to be nice to everyone and not to tell anyone my business." Being "nice to everyone" is what produces the immensely attractive surface of Southern life, that faultless politeness and sweetness that you can still encounter often enough in Milledgeville. Yet it is a politeness that engulfs every other emotion, that permits no contact on any but the most superficial levels. And it is not merely a graciousness that is carted out for strangers. It seems to exist between mothers and daughters, husbands and wives. It seems everywhere to substitute "doing pretty" for genuine warmth. It censures all of those excesses of feeling that would constitute "fussing" and prohibits being close enough to anyone to tell them your "business."

But what if one's "business," one's most essential feelings are not the stuff pretty gestures are made of? What if, from girlhood, you have known you loathe the Southern belle you are supposed to become? What if you have felt "other" and "different" in a milieu that is horribly embarrassed by anything unconventional? And what if your business later on is dying slowly, being filled with impotent rage at your own weakness? And what if, through it all, no one will even tolerate your "fussing" about it?

Like the tight-lipped kids in her books, Flannery O'Connor, I suspect, told her "business" to no one. She rather retreated from it herself into the role of a Georgia farmer-wit. It is not surprising that after a particularly horrible bout of her disease, she would paint a portrait of herself next to a peacock looking like a suffering, proud adolescent in a wide straw hat. Like Mrs. Hopewell in "Good Country People," who thinks of her daughter as a child because it is too painful to think of her as a thirty-two-year-old Ph.D. who has had a weak heart and a wooden leg for twenty years, O'Connor seems to have found a way out of her unpretty situation by denying it. Flannery O'Connor seems to have lived out a fiction and written down her life.

The fiction O'Connor lived had its roots in that Southern need to do pretty regardless of what you feel, and in her own remarkable ability to divorce behavior from feeling and even to conceal feelings from herself. Much as she hated the Mrs. Hopewells, Mrs. Mays, and Mrs. Turpins she wrote about, she was, in many ways, like them. She denied in her own life what they denied in the lives of their daughters and sons. She seems to have made a peculiar arrangement with existence in which she found an acceptable alternative to the Southern Belle in a variety of roles, ranging from the witty hick to the uncompromising Catholic. She seems to have gone through the motions of conventional behavior without becoming deeply involved in the conventional world around her and without expecting any deep human contact. She was compliant, affirmative, happy with farm life, an excellent daughter, a Catholic unresentful of death—she was cheerful; but she seems to have been oddly out of touch with those more essential feelings that explode in her work. And it is through her very ability to detach herself from those feelings that she came closest to being what she had never admired: a Southern Lady.

Milledgeville is publicly proud of Regina Cline O'Connor's daughter. In the public library you will find a memorial display of her work accompanied by a vase of peacock feathers and a curiously out-of-place painting O'Connor did of an enraged rooster. Freshmen at her alma mater (which has, since O'Connor's time, changed its name and admitted men) are required to read her work. Yet despite the outward display and approval, you will find that almost no one withdraws her books from the library and few people buy them. When they do it is usually as gifts for people up North or out of town. They ship them off as genuine Milledgeville products often because Atlanta critics or Northern "interleckschuls" have said they are admirable. Many who have read some of O'Connor's work do not read more. They apologize for not being more "literary" and explain that they cannot rid themselves of the feeling that there is something very "peculiar" about it, something very "different."

For many who knew her, Flannery O'Connor *was* "different." There is, in the memory of one Milledgeville matron, the image of O'Connor at nineteen or twenty who, when invited to a wedding shower for an old family friend, remained standing, her back pressed against the wall, scowling at the group of women who had sat down to lunch. Neither the devil nor her mother could make her say yes to this fiercely gracious female society, but Flannery O'Connor could not say no even in a whisper. She could not refuse the invitation but she would not accept it either. She did not exactly "fuss" but neither did she "do pretty." Perhaps the essence of Flannery O'Connor is there in that mute scowl. To borrow one of her lines, maybe that is what made her "different."

The great strength of O'Connor's fiction seems to me to spring from the silent and remote rage that erupts from the quiet surface of her stories and that so unexpectedly explodes. It appears, for example, when the Misfit with great politeness has the family exterminated, or when he answers the grandmother's "niceness" with a gunshot and thereby suggests that neither Christian charity nor South-

ern politeness can contain all the darker human impulses.
It appears again in the punishment of the vain, self-satisfied
Mrs. Turpin, who gets a book thrown at her. Perhaps it
has a quieter voice in those sweetly nasty comments Mrs.
Turpin's Negroes make as they talk among themselves to
comfort her: "You the sweetest lady I know." "She pretty
too." "And stout." And perhaps it is there in the impulses
of all those resentful sons and daughters in the pages of
Flannery O'Connor's fiction who are frozen in an extended, rebellious adolescence where, in a perpetual dependency because of illness or fear, the price they ought to
pay for being cared for is silence, acquiescence to an effective, controlling, exasperatingly polite, and very removed
mother.

Perhaps there is something of this rage even in O'Connor's love for peacocks. Did she admire the ease with
which they gobbled up all the flowers in sight, destroying
her mother's flower beds and covering the lawn with droppings? Were those majestic birds that broke all the rules
what Flannery O'Connor wanted to be? Yet the curse on
the bird is its yowl—its ugly voice that makes it most beautiful when silent, a voice that to Flannery O'Connor
sounded like "cheers for an invisible parade."[2] Was that
invisible parade the procession of misfits, prophets, and
lonely and murderous children who unleash their violence
so freely in the fiction of Flannery O'Connor?

Flannery O'Connor never yowled in public. She never
gave voice to whatever her mute scowl expressed. In reading her opinions and observations in the Fitzgeralds' edition
of her occasional prose, I am struck by how little she actually says. There is little in these uninspired talks and comments on writing to suggest the strength or power of her
own fiction. Her statements of intention have so little to do
with her work that Lawrence's dictum, "Never trust the

teller; trust the tale," often comes to mind. "The Fiction
Writer and His Country," for example, has done more to
mislead readers than to inform them. O'Connor says, "I see
from the standpoint of Christian orthodoxy. This means
that for me the meaning of life is centered in our Redemption by Christ and that what I see in the world, I see in its
relation to that."[3]

That O'Connor's work has so often been seen as merely
polemic is largely due to such statements about her own
belief and the willingness of critics to accept her statements
of intention as accurate descriptions of her art.

Although I do not question the faith of Flannery O'Connor, it seems to me odd that she would so freely admit she
had the conscience of a Catholic, and do so much to deny
she had the impulses of a sinner. I do not think her faith
can be divorced from the context of her life, a life where
outward compliance and external order seem to have been
achieved only through detachment from inner turmoil. It
is at least a possibility that her religion provided a legiti-
mate sanction for violent and destructive impulses, impulses which became acceptable when they were called
righteous and directed at the "godless." Religion could
have been an effective way to both express and contain
fury of a very irreligious kind. In any event, O'Connor's
assertions of Christian orthodoxy do not accurately describe her art. They are belied by the human experience in
her work. Nevertheless, encouraged by O'Connor's decla-
mations of faith, critics so diverse as the indefatigable Sister
M. Bernetta Quinn and Stanley Edgar Hyman explained
her work as so much new exegesis on traditional Christian
theology.

In general, O'Connor's short stories have been viewed as
vignettes about the search for redemption in Christ. Her
novels are seen—most notably by Stanley Edgar Hyman—

as similar quests which also involve the hero's recognition of his vocation and end in his ordination. For example, Sister Bertrande Meyers[4] writes only about the effects of redemptive grace in O'Connor's fiction and Bob Dowell reduces the action of her stories to a common sequence: an initial rebellion against belief, a crisis of faith, and a resolution in a moment of grace.[5] Albert Griffith discusses how such figures as Shiftlet, Guizac, and Star Drake partake of the Mystical Body and share a vocation to live the spiritual life.[6] Sister Bernetta Quinn finds that each story in *A Good Man Is Hard to Find*, "whether by explication or implication,"[7] embodies a sacrament—a visible sign of invisible grace. Sister Mariella Gable goes so far as to claim O'Connor's fiction is an embodiment of the ecumenical spirit of the second Vatican council.[8] In his lengthy essay *Flannery O'Connor*, Robert Drake claims O'Connor saw herself as an evangelist who had come "to call the wicked to repentance." He thinks "Jesus Christ is finally the principal character in all Miss O'Connor's fiction . . . and her heroes' confrontation with Him is the one story she keeps telling over and over again."[9]

Because I think O'Connor told more than religious tales, I propose to view her fiction not for the dogma it illustrates, but for the themes it suggests. To assume that her work is merely a monologue on redemption is to see it only in part, to ignore much of its meaning, and to lose sight of the believer behind the belief. My own feeling is that O'Connor never merely wrote about Redemption, but that the very act of writing was itself a redemptive process for her. It may have been the only, and perhaps unconscious, way she could express all the contradictions within her.

While I shall continue to remind the reader of the usual interpretations of her work, I do not think O'Connor's fiction can be explained by her Catholicism alone. Nor have the few critics who have said that her work is not religious ever fully said what it is. Irving Howe has mentioned her orthodoxy as only one aspect of her work, the French novelist, J. M. G. Le Clézio, sees her as a writer of existential tales of initiation, and her sometime correspondent John Hawkes goes so far as to say that her Catholicism and moral bias disappear in the creative process.

As Howe says, O'Connor

> could bring into play resources of worldliness such as one might find in the work of a good many sophisticated modern writers. . . . Except for an occasional phrase, which serves partly as a rhetorical signal that more than ordinary verisimilitude is at stake, there are no unavoidable pressures to consider these stories in a strictly religious sense. They stand securely on their own, as renderings and criticisms of human experience.[10]

Le Clézio, perhaps less awed than his American counterparts by the existence of a Catholic writer, sees O'Connor's work as rendering the most painful and profound of human experiences, growing up. Writing about *The Violent Bear It Away*, one of the more peculiar novels of initiation, he says that the fight between Rayber, a well-meaning atheist, and Tarwater, the fanatic old prophet, over the baptism of Rayber's idiot son is not a struggle between faith and reason but a fight against "la vacance, l'inutilisation." As he says:

> Pour lutter contre ce climat funeste, les hommes se tournent vers la jeunesse, vers l'enfance, vers la naissance. Il s'agit de se les approprier. Blasphématoire ou bien sacramentel, le baptême est l'acte le plus important. C'est l'acte de propriété par excellence, celui qui extirpe du néant, qui signe qui fait naître une deuxième fois.[11]

In their struggle to possess the idiot child, both Rayber and Tarwater fight against their own pervasive feeling of nothingness, a feeling that can only be reduced by violently affirming their own existence. The brutal baptism erupts from a confused desire for meaning and culminates in the acquisition of another person. In this novel's chain of human cruelty, the strong acquire the weak and the weak acquire the weakest. As old Tarwater once captured *him* in his infancy, so young Tarwater grows up to "engulf" or destroy a defenseless idiot child to assert himself. In O'Connor's world, so irreducibly concrete, the modes of destruction and assertion are always described externally or, to borrow Wyndham Lewis' phrase, soullessly and deadly by their frontal lines and masses.

Baptism, an act symbolizing the transcendence of the body, is used to establish how much of a material commodity the body is. It becomes the supreme act of property in which young Tarwater and the idiot are, in turn, acquired and used to advance the cause of the old prophet. In simultaneously baptizing and murdering the idiot, Young Tarwater turns him into a tool he uses to destroy his attachment to both Rayber and the old prophet. Baptism is connected with the boy's rejection of spiritual life and human ties. It expresses his need to escape from the men who would make him a theological man—whether as prophet or atheist. It expresses more a human dilemma than a need for the sublime. As John Hawkes has noticed, there is very little emphasis on the soul, the mind, or any other form of transcendent reality in O'Connor's work. He thinks that O'Connor committed herself creatively to characters who have no soul, no transcendent quality. As he says,

The point is that in the most vigorously moral of writers the actual creation of fiction seems to depend on immoral impulse. . . . My own feeling is that just as the creative process threatens the holy throughout Flannery O'Connor's fiction, . . . so too throughout this fiction, the creative process transforms the writer's objective Catholic knowledge of the devil into an authorial attitude in itself in some measure diabolical . . . the disbelief that we breathe in with the air of the times emerges fully as two-sided or complex as attraction for the holy.[12]

By "diabolic," I think Hawkes means reductive or mechanical. He sees this diabolism in both her style and her characterization. Her "one-cylinder syntax" or "good country talk" is a way of exploiting the "demolishing syntax of the devil," creating a flat language expressive of the flat personalities she creates.

Hawkes does not go far enough. I think O'Connor is best when writing like a devil of reduction, most convincing when most literal and least convincing when consciously symbolic. In Hawkes's words, in the process of using the devil's voice for satire, O'Connor becomes the devil herself, speaking most authentically when using his voice. In effect this destroys the balance between the satiric and the real, the literal and metaphoric, the actual and symbolic. Consequently, much of O'Connor's work tends to remain literal and never reach a symbolic or even allegoric plane. While some of her suns become Eucharistic, most of them remain merely suns or are reduced to "fat yellow roosts" with chickens on them. The latter is the symbolizing process in reverse: a foreshortening of meaning that reduces significance instead of expanding it. What is immense and expansive is made to appear minute. O'Connor creates a language for a universe filled with shrunken objects, smelling remarkably like a chicken coop. This whittling, abrasive impulse is much more than a vagary of literary style; it is one of the most powerful and most ignored expressions of O'Connor's relation to her work and of the quality of life in her fiction.

Such imbalance between the literal and metaphoric is due less to a precarious style than to O'Connor's attempt to straddle two views of life: one traditionally Christian, the other modern and secular. Her work may be seen as a transition between the older forms of allegory and symbolism which describe a traditional, Christian universe of depth and significance and the newer objectivism whose most vocal advocates have been Alain Robbe-Grillet in France and Susan Sontag in the United States. O'Connor is not so extreme a symbolist as William Faulkner in, for example, *Absalom, Absalom!* nor is she so "objective" as Alain Robbe-Grillet in *Last Year at Marienbad* or Susan Sontag in *Death Kit.* Nor do I think it is relevant here to describe exhaustively either literary style, since it is merely to define more clearly the direction of O'Connor's work that I mention the poles it swings between before showing where it comes to rest.

The symbolist novel, the novel of James Joyce, Virginia Woolf, and William Faulkner, to name a few of its practitioners, renders the stream of thoughts and feelings below the level of speech or action. It replaces a concern for character and plot with the texture of consciousness itself— with the play of images across the mind, or the memory of significant things, feelings, or events. In the absence of traditional treatment of character and plot, the development of the novel depends on the recurrence of particular images or thoughts which expand in meaning and grow into symbols as the novel progresses. To put it simply, the novel is "symbolic" because the "real" world of concrete objects, specific actions, and individual personality is used mainly to give life to a wealth of intangible meanings, or to provide a focus or center which can give form and coherence to a swarm of impressions. The concrete object or experience becomes a core around which consciousness reverberates. For example, the actual lighthouse in Woolf's *To the Lighthouse*—its height, color, location—is less important than the significance it has for everyone in the novel. The same is true of Sutpen's plantation in *Absalom, Absalom!* In a similar way, the real circumstances of Joe Christmas' birth in *Light in August* are irrelevant to the meaning his birth comes to have for him and for the novel. In the symbolist novel, the reality of the concrete event or object keeps disappearing into its significance. The concrete reality is always transcended by the significance it generates, a significance that can be so varied and complex that it eludes any one definition.[13]

Sontag and Robbe-Grillet admire a very different kind of art, one which does much to avoid the inner psychological world of the symbolist novel and to do away with the universe of deep, expansive meanings it describes. Objective art is largely an art of surface reality. It is essentially an art of literalization, of stripping away the connotative, symbolic values of words, things, and events in order to expose the concrete object or event language denotes. For example, if Faulkner's Joe Christmas could ever be a character in an objective novel, he would never be seen as a black Christ crucified and apotheosized as he is in *Light in August*. He would be a man who might be a mulatto, who by chance murdered Joanna Burden, who was himself murdered, who remained dead, and who happened to have had the name "Christmas." The emphasis would not be on the inner life of the man nor on the significance he has for others. It would be focused clearly on the external facts of his life and death. Objective art owes little to Freud, something to the psychology of Sartre, and most to phenomenologists like Husserl and Heidegger. If the symbolist novel moves toward the transcendent, the abstract, or the mythic, the objective novel could be said to move in the opposite direction toward the concrete, the photographic, or the cinematic.

In an effort to avoid abstract meanings, the objective novel will, as in Robbe-Grillet's *Last Year at Marienbad*, dwell on endless lists and descriptions of furniture or random objects. Characters who live among these objects seem to merge with them; they are described as though they themselves are objects who have no capacity for introspection or feeling, but have the power to see, to walk, and to act. What they see, say, and do is never supposed to develop expansive meanings.

In "A Future for the Novel" Robbe-Grillet rejects the older "world of depth signification (psychological, social, functional)" in favor of a universe that simply is. The physical presence of objects defines, by the sheer weight of their own substance, the whole of reality. As he says,

> Let it be first of all by their presence that objects and gestures establish themselves, and let this presence continue to prevail over whatever explanatory theory may try to enclose them in a system of references, whether emotional, sociological, Freudian, or metaphysical.[14]

Robbe-Grillet arrives at his belief that the object or gesture should always be greater than its ideological context by a laborious mental process. Flannery O'Connor may never have thought about it at all. Yet she created an art that is, in many instances, as emotionally flat as Robbe-Grillet's, an art where object and gesture simply *are*. In Flannery O'Connor's most powerful fiction, to paraphrase William Carlos Williams, there are no ideas about things, there are only the things themselves.[15]

As I will show, because life offers no spirit, mind, soul, or any transcendent quality in O'Connor's fiction, the shape of a man limits and defines him. He can never be more than his bodily substance. The stories of *A Good Man Is Hard To Find* all explore the relation of the physical to the transcendent, the body to the mind. In varying degrees the spiritual is destroyed by the overwhelming presence of the material world. Intangibles such as emotion, significance, or abstract meaning are, in effect, trapped within objects or within men who are treated as objects. Consequently, the stories show no revelation of states of mind, no psychological analysis, and no interior monologue. Like one of her characters, O'Connor does not care about the "underhead." She shows no "stream" or continuum of consciousness but, instead, simplifies complex feelings and objectifies psychological states. There is often so little continuity between feeling and action that they seem very distinct phenomena. For example, self-hatred or desire to commit suicide will appear as the murder of another person, usually the hero's double. When this occurs, as it does in *Wise Blood* when Motes murders his double, Solace Layfield, even the feeling of satisfaction Motes has at ridding himself of Layfield is objectified. It is Motes's car, the Essex that ran over Layfield, that seems pleased and not Motes himself. In "The Life You Save May Be Your Own," Shiftlet does not feel hatred for himself for abandoning his mother-in-law and defenseless wife, he becomes enraged at the hitch-hiking boy because the boy ran away from his mother. O'Connor's characters are, in general, so estranged from their emotional life that they feel their emotions do not even belong to them. They seem to belong to someone else, a stranger who is, nevertheless oddly familiar; a double who, in some way, recapitulates their own experience. Her heroes are so emotionally dead that they can perform the most outrageous acts without any conscious awareness of feelings of elation or despair. It is not surprising that the Misfit corrects his comment that there's "no pleasure but meanness," with "It's no real pleasure in life." Believing that the only relation possible between men and between men and things is "strangeness," Robbe-Grillet claims to record the distance between objects and reified men without an emotional sense of loss. While O'Connor sometimes achieves a similar detachment in isolated scenes, she usually displays a certain joy in human isolation, a perverse relish for it. She may resemble Robbe-Grillet in style, create characters as emotionally flat as his, and stress the mechanical quality of life, but she never merely reproduces a neutral universe or records the distance between men. O'Connor does not reflect the real world; she reduces it.

Many of O'Connor's stories move by a process of constriction in which abstract, spiritual, or expansive longings shrink into a concrete act, an act that is with remarkable frequency akin to murder or suicide. Since she never treats interiors of thought or feeling, these acts are forced to bear the entire meaning of the story. As I have suggested, they are usually effected quietly and without apparent emotion. Yet, as the discussions that follow will suggest, action erupts from an emotional void so frequently in O'Connor's work that you are forced to see the peculiar combination as one of her preoccupations.

Action without feeling seems to have had a unique significance for O'Connor. What it may have meant for her is implied in "A Memoir for Mary Ann," an essay she wrote for the Sisters of Our Lady of Perpetual Help Free Cancer Home to introduce their biography of a child who came to their home in Atlanta at three with half her face "straight and bright" and the other half missing an eye and crowded with tumors. She died there at twelve. The order was founded by Nathaniel Hawthorne's daughter, Rose, who devoted her life to caring for people no one else would care for. Yet it is obviously Rose's father who fascinates O'Connor. She dwells at length on Hawthorne's fictional account of his meeting with an "awful-looking rheumy child" in a Liverpool workhouse who stood in front of him in a "mute appeal to be held." Hawthorne's character is "shy of actual contact with human beings, afflicted with a peculiar distaste for whatever was ugly, and furthermore, accustomed to that habit of observation from an insulated standpoint which is said . . . to have the tendency of putting ice into the blood." O'Connor goes on to relate the incident as it appeared in Hawthorne's notebooks. Like Hawthorne, she was morally opposed to "ice in the blood." Yet it is ice in the blood and the fear of it that is one of her greatest and most authentic subjects.

Fearing that he lacked compassion, Hawthorne embraced the child. O'Connor explains, "The ice in the blood which he feared, and which this very fear preserved him from, was turned by [Rose] into . . . warmth. If he observed fearfully but truthfully; if he acted reluctantly but firmly, she charged ahead, secure in the path his truthfulness had outlined for her."

O'Connor has an astonishing ability to ignore the essential feelings of the man who observed from a distance, who acted out of an assertion of will and not out of any genuine warmth. Perhaps by default, she admired his action and obscured his coldness, preferring to believe that simply the fear of "ice in the blood" could melt it. In the absence of positive feeling, it is only action or external gesture that can redeem you from emotional death, from "ice in the blood" and the fear of it. Hawthorne's action produces a semblance of warmth, a kind of compassion that brings him closer to the child and the suffering humanity the child may represent. O'Connor's actions do not.

O'Connor's heroes rarely want to feel compassion because they fear human contact more than they fear emotional death. As the discussions that follow will show, in the absence of emotion, action becomes the primary sign of life. But it signals a life based on repudiation of human contact and on rejection of any desire for it. O'Connor's heroes can never connect with themselves or with others. They come closest in momentary acts of violence in which they murder or commit suicide. For the duration of the destructive act, for the moment in which they annihilate some human tie, they are able to come most powerfully alive, to transcend the otherwise engulfing emotional "ice." Yet O'Connor reduces and diminishes the significance of their acts by a variety of stylistic devices. As I have said, she not only simplifies and objectifies her hero's psychological state at the moment of his most "passionate" act, she places that act near the end of her story, where it expresses the final step in the progressive reduction of symbolic meanings. Her reductive impulse is embedded in the structure of her stories, which, in general, move from the symbolic toward the objective.

Writing within an older literary framework of traditional symbols, she begins with a vague suggestion of depth that is not sufficiently developed to make her work symbolic but does provide a point of departure—a three-dimensional image which she can flatten out as the story progresses. For example, as I will show in my discussion of "The Life You Save May Be Your Own," Shiftlet, that man of spirit, first appears as a silhouette of a crooked cross against the sunset and becomes simply a crook as the story unfolds. Similarly, O'Connor will often begin with an abstraction or metaphor that becomes more and more concrete as she continues. This is a way of destroying the significance of symbols, of making them specific and concrete or, in other words, of making the spiritual physical or the abstract literal. F. W. Dupee has called this technique "comic literalization" in his essay on *Zuleika Dobson*, where he describes it as the power of words to become things, to materialize in specific action. As he says,

> The casual wish is father to the deed on an unprecedented scale. The cliché bears watching lest it come true with a vengeance. In Zuleika's career the literalizing principle is writ large. . . . She is a *femme fatale* whose brief stay at Oxford has been actually fatal to hundreds.[16]

Less comically employed, the literalizing principle controls the organization of many of O'Connor's stories. Beginning with a metaphoric statement, the story develops as the metaphor becomes realized in a concrete action or material object. For example, "The River" opens with Mrs. Connin and child "going to the river to a healing," where they will be among the baptized, members of the visible church of Christ. The river, as the preacher says, is the baptismal place where sin is washed away and heaven is seen. Taking the metaphor of baptism as admission to the visible church of Christ literally, the child "intended . . . to keep on going this time until he found the Kingdom of Christ in the river." What he finds there is death. The story closes with the preacher's realization that the child has drowned himself and the awareness that all his metaphors of Christ's healing river have their source in the ultimate concretion, mortality.

O'Connor not only destroys all transcendent qualities by burying them in the body, she regards the body itself as repulsive. In her love for the material, her obsession with animal reality—perhaps best shown by the ubiquitous hogs that fill her world—she resembles the creators of what has been called the literature of disgust, best known from the work of William Burroughs and Hubert Selby, Jr. Considering the absence of visceral prose in O'Connor's work, such a comparison may seem unlikely at first. Yet her work has a similar impulse and direction. Burroughs' image of ultimate reality—the junkie naked in the sunlight—is not unlike Mrs. Turpin's final vision of her pigs luminous at sunset. The body variously injected with sperm, heroin, and methodone, ejecting urine, sweat, vomit, and feces, resembles O'Connor's less visceral bodies leaning on machines —wooden legs, orthopedic shoes, dental braces, hearing aids, and those innumerable props which come to dominate rather than support human life. Burroughs, Selby, and O'Connor write about people trapped within their own bodies, figuratively drowning in their own juices. O'Connor describes visually what they describe tactilely and, substituting an obsession for violence and religion for their concern with sex and drugs, makes a similar statement in a less "sensuous" way. Like so many American writers of the last century, O'Connor substitutes a concern for deformity, murder, and religion for violent sexuality. In this she is traditional, but the affectless, mechanical quality of violence in her world, and the lack of profound human involvement, give her work a peculiar modernity. While the primary themes of her fiction are traditional and justify Howe's opinion of her work as a description of general human experience and Le Clézio's definition of that experience as both growing up and seeking to define the self against the abyss, O'Connor's development of what could be called the affectless grotesque makes her work remarkably new.

The opening paragraphs of her first book, *Wise Blood*, suggest the theme she develops over and over in her later work. Hazel Motes's double glance defines her line of vision: he looks out the window of a moving train, wanting to jump, and then back toward the end of the car at a Negro porter who claims to be from Chicago, the son of a railroad man, but who Haze is sure is the son of a Parrum "nigger who got the cholera from a pig." In other words, one can look out at a present that is nothingness and chaos or back at one's physical origins, sharing the fortunes and diseases of life with a pig. Haze is momentarily immobilized between the prospects of the window and the porter. The present and the future for him are a landscape blurred by speed, involving a possible leap into nothingness; the past provides greater stability and the security of a known phenomenon but its phenomena are always varieties of the more painful human experiences: disease, decay, and death.

This conflict, most generally stated as one between the present and the past, appears in all O'Connor's work in different forms: psychological, social, religious. Its recurrence contributes to a body of work of remarkable uniformity and persistent design. O'Connor consistently expresses her themes as conflicts or embodies them in images of opposites. Whether she exalts her alienated hero (as she does in "A Temple of the Holy Ghost") or burlesques him (as she does Motes in *Wise Blood*), all her heroes alternate between the same peculiar, almost contradictory forces: emotional death and violence, confusion and certainty, detachment from human contact and domination by it. Before discussing O'Connor's fiction in detail, I should like briefly to survey the conflicts, images, and themes that preoccupy her.

Strife can appear as the discord between generations, as it does so frequently in *Everything That Rises Must Converge* and in a few of the stories in *A Good Man Is Hard to Find*. Here it has a psychological bent as O'Connor's thirtyish adolescents do battle with their old mothers. In the novels and in many of the stories, it finds a social and religious expression as a conflict between a secular, relativistic sense of life in which man is perfectible through reason and technology, and a religious belief in absolutes in which human evil and human suffering are unredeemable. The conflict between a secular and a religious sense of life appears in nearly all O'Connor's fiction, but it is expressed most powerfully when it is added to a social conflict between rural and urban life.

O'Connor's backwoods abound in "holy" men who find freedom and detachment there. In isolated farms or on lonely back roads they can unleash their fury unchecked. Like Parzival's forest, her wilderness is both a state of mind and the literal home of religious experience; a place where the power of the past over the present, the old over the young, is absolute. Old Tarwater takes his grand-nephew from Rayber's house in the city to raise him in a wilderness where he can mold the boy in his own image. Johnson in "The Lame Shall Enter First" is raised by his grandfather, who lives in the hills with a "remnant" which has gone to "bury some Bibles in a cave and take two of different kinds of animals and all that. Like Noah." And the Misfit performs his mass murder far from the "Authorities." Yet all these "holy" men have come to the wilderness to escape the optimistic and hopeful world of the town, a world that terrifies them with its ambiguities.

Through O'Connor's cities stalk those *bêtes noires* she loves to thwart, the social worker and the teacher who advocate the examined life, human commitments, and the bonds of human compassion. Sheppard, the social worker in "The Lame Shall Enter First" and Rayber, the schoolteacher in *The Violent Bear It Away* epitomize a secular, "humanistic" spirit shared by a number of characters in the canon who are neither city dwellers, teachers, nor social workers but who are loving and optimistic, if somewhat self-satisfied.[17] On a smaller scale, they mirror the struggle of Rayber with Tarwater, Sheppard with Johnson, and the Misfit with the Authorities. Since the conflict occurs in so many of O'Connor's stories, I should like to outline it once in its most extreme form to avoid repetition.

Rayber and Sheppard are secular missionaries who see technology and psychology as roads to salvation in secular terms: health and happiness. They oppose a flexible, relative notion of illness and health to Tarwater's and Johnson's rigid sense of damnation and sanctity. Sheppard befriends young Johnson, seeing his religious obsession as the result of his grandfather's domination, his lack of psychosocial development, and his lameness. He tries to win the boy's friendship, interest him in space travel instead of religion, and buy him an orthopedic shoe to correct his limp. But Johnson "knows" he is evil and not simply misguided. And Johnson remains unimpressed. "It don't matter if he's good," he says to Sheppard's son, "He ain't *right.*" And so Johnson refuses the shoe and corrupts Sheppard's son.

O'Connor reserves her greatest venom for Rayber, whose passionate devotion to his idiot son, Bishop, and whose longing to become a father to young Tarwater she thwarts. Rayber comes to represent for O'Connor the horrors of human tenderness, of a flexible ambiguous conception of goodness, and of the terror unleashed by introspection. Rayber epitomizes O'Connor's conception of the "interleckschul," thoughtful, introspective, obsessed with a variety of human involvements. He is one of her greatest villains largely, it seems, because he inflicted a psychiatric explanation of behavior on the old prophet.

Rayber writes an article on Tarwater in which he explains the old man's religiosity as originating in "insecurity." Tarwater does not realize that he is reading about himself until he sees Rayber smile. Rayber's ambiguous smile unleashes on the prophet all the forces of complexity, of insecurity and doubt. And in O'Connor's world doubt and complexity can kill. Old Tarwater "felt he was tied hand and foot inside the schoolteacher's head. . . . Jonah, Ezekiel, Daniel, he was at that moment all of them—the swallowed, the lowered, the enclosed" (V, 348). When Rayber offers him consolation, saying "you've got to be born again by your own efforts, back to the real world where there's no savior but yourself," Tarwater is enraged. He scrawls on the back of Rayber's article: "THE PROPHET I RAISE UP OUT OF THIS BOY WILL BURN YOUR EYES CLEAN." He kidnaps young Tarwater and flees into the wilderness.

Tarwater cannot recognize himself in Rayber's portrait, where is neither God nor Satan, Good nor Evil, but merely human. Rayber's thought processes make him feel trapped, lowered, swallowed, enclosed, dead. Introspection for Tarwater will lead to death, to the annihilation of a life he insists has divine sanction. He has already been "redeemed" through *avoiding* his "underhead," through staying on the surface of himself, through following the will of God, who speaks to him through wonderfully unambiguous signs. His freedom lies in his ability to detach himself from human problems, human emotions, and human involvements. His freedom lies in his ability simply to act.

The image of Tarwater locked and bound in Rayber's head defines the fate of O'Connor's heroes. The mere fact of being thought about—of entering the mind of another person—engulfs them in an unwanted human contact. All become victims of the compassion, the abstractions, the ambiguities of the modern world Rayber represents. Doubt and uncertainty terrify them and drive them to violence until one by one, they are literally confined and pinioned by the larger social world. Tarwater has spent four years in a mental hospital, the Misfit has been imprisoned, Johnson has been in reform school, and Hazel Motes falls prey to the police. And all because they are "different."

Their "difference" lies partly in their overwhelming fear of ambiguity, confusion, and disorder. The Misfit does not know whether God exists or Christ "did what he said" and literally raised the dead. "If I had of been there I would of known," he says, "and I wouldn't be like I am now [a Misfit], because I can't make what all I done wrong fit what all I gone through in punishment" (G, 28-29).

The Misfit's "punishment" is being the captive audience of a psychiatric explanation of his crime. As he says, "It was a head-doctor at the penitentiary said what I had done was kill my daddy but I known that for a lie. My daddy died in nineteen ought nineteen of the epidemic flu and I never had a thing to do with it" (G, 26). He cannot remember killing his "father" and is as confused by the head-doctor's account of his crime as Tarwater was by Rayber's psychologizing. (He does, of course, kill a woman who calls him one of her babies and who represents all the forces of society, tradition, and family.) Like Tarwater, the Misfit describes both his confusion and entrapment as being buried alive. His cell, like Rayber's head, is a coffin where truth becomes very elusive. "Turn to the left, it was a wall. Look up it was a ceiling, look down it was a floor. I forget what I done, lady. You can do one thing or you can do another, kill a man or take a tire off his car, because sooner or later you're going to forget what it was you done and just be punished for it" (G, 25-26).

The themes of entrapment and confusion have their source in the pervasive emotional death of O'Connor's heroes. The Misfit has so blocked any connection to other men that he could not remember if he killed a man or stole his tire. Both murder and theft are engulfed in a general meaninglessness, a confusion so cosmic that there is no escape from it in thought, no way to order it logically. For both Tarwater and the Misfit, the experience of other people or even of themselves—of questioning their own motives—is like dying, like being engulfed in an unfathomable morass. Old Tarwater, locked in Rayber's head or confined in the pit of the asylum, and the Misfit in his coffin-cell are metaphors for their relation to society: they are both ostracized by it and engulfed by it, unable to accept it or to withstand it.

Nor is O'Connor's wrath limited to jails and mental hospitals. Organized churches, both Protestant and Catholic, are often described as extensions of secular society. For example, in "A Temple of the Holy Ghost" the convent is viewed ironically and, in imagery, associated with the goals of the Raybers and Sheppards. Like Settembrini's imagined utopia, it has succeeded in eliminating pain and suffering. The religious heroes of the story are a homely child and a hermaphrodite who works with a carnival and gives his own quasi-religious freak show in the woods on the edge of town. The only crucifixion that is real to O'Connor is the one a freak lives out daily for a lifetime.

These are O'Connor's heroes, the saints and martyrs of her fictive world. They are generally murderers, psychic cripples, sometimes freaks, always brutal men who have a sense of sin and think about God, sometimes. The Misfit's despair, murder of his "father," and imprisonment suggest one of O'Connor's pervasive metaphors for life: a prison in which man suffers for a crime he cannot remember. From a theological point of view, the crime may be original sin. But from a human standpoint, it is "ice in the blood."

O'Connor's heroes have lost all sense of human kinship. Some, like Tarwater, feel they are incarnations of righteousness free to create and destroy at will. Having taken the right to act as inexplicably as God, O'Connor's hero finds himself in godlike isolation, alien to human suffering and joy. He can kill without pleasure or remorse. At best, like Shiftlet or Motes, he can feel love for a machine. Reaching a state of ultimate human indifference, he achieves the state of Querry in Graham Greene's *A Burnt-Out Case*.[18]

> She struck him in the face, but he felt the blow no more than a dab of butter against his cheek. He said, "I am sorry, I am too far gone. I can't feel at all. I am a leper."

In O'Connor's heroes, the disease of life has also run its course, rotted all it could, and left only an insensate, durable core of hate. Having emerged from the asylum and prison, Tarwater and the Misfit wreak their vengeance on society.

If violence in the social realist novels in the Thirties reflected the horror of life in Marxist terms, violence in O'Connor's work reflects a more modern brutality. O'Connor's most violent men have been so crushed by life that they suffer with remarkable passivity the alarming pity or open contempt of a society that does not value the "sanctity" of hermaphrodites or psychic freaks. They can never fully shout out their rage at any of the Authorities who shut them up in asylums, jails, or on isolated farms; who demand they analyze themselves, and whose pity or compassion render them still more impotent. It is only in acts of violence that they give voice to their mute fury.

Even in their violence O'Connor's heroes are estranged from their inmost rage. O'Connor always gives their fury a detached, oblique quality. The Misfit, for example, murders a woman who calls him "one of her babies" and who represents all the forces of Southern tradition and society. Yet he "does pretty" throughout the mass murder. He speaks politely and murders the grandmother after declaring there was no finer woman than his mother. Similarly, in O'Connor's brilliant story, "Revelation," Mary Grace tolerates her mother in a polite silence while she grows more and more enraged by her mother's double, Mrs. Turpin. Violence toward a stranger lets both misfits express their fury and remain detached from its source at the same time. It both expresses and controls their anger.

Violence springs out of an immense, chaotic inner rage and imposes a kind of order on it. In a sense O'Connor's heroes murder to create order, justice, and equilibrium. As the Misfit put it, to "make what all I done wrong" equal to "what all I gone through in punishment." His murder not only equalizes his crimes and his punishment, it establishes many kinds of order. The Misfit's murder proves that he has resolved his doubts about whether Christ raised the dead. He confronts his own uncertainty with an absolute, irrevocable act. Similarly Motes kills Layfield, who has a wife, six children, and tuberculosis and who impersonates Motes in order to earn three dollars. He parodies Motes's sanctity out of necessity and not conviction. By killing the false image of himself, or perhaps an aspect of himself that acts out of sheer self-interest, Motes remains the only true prophet. Similarly by drowning Bishop, young Tarwater tries to prove he is free from both his uncles; by corrupting Norton, Johnson tries to prove to Sheppard that his grandfather was right—he is evil and damned and not simply misguided. Demanding neither hope nor salvation, O'Connor's heroes need only certainty. And all they can know absolutely, "know for sure," is isolation, rage, and death.

O'Connor's hero comes most alive as he liberates his otherwise passive and silent rage. He tries to murder his way out of his own abyss, to escape, through moments of self-transcendence in violence, the pervasive feeling of nothingness. At the moment of his most brutal act, he is able to break with a past in which he has been despised, scorned, and ostracized. If he is unable to understand the symbolic verbal world around him, he is able to answer it in a concrete act of repudiation. He imposes a kind of simplicity on the confusion about him, certainty on a time of flexible truths, a floodlight on a kaleidoscope. He hacks a kind of value out of a world where value is all too elusive—a value that, emerging from his own experience, is invariably an affirmation of hate, destruction, and revenge.

Confusion and certainty, alienation and violence appear together in style as well as in theme. O'Connor's style often conflicts with the action she describes and reflects both the emotional flatness of her work and its theme of affectless violence. For example, rigid and stereotyped language often describes the most chaotic, extraordinary events. The Misfit's language abounds in the phrases of politeness: "Yes mam," "I pre-chate that, lady," "Nome," "Would you mind stepping back in them woods there with them?," "I'm sorry I don't have on a shirt before you ladies," and "I'll look and see terrectly." His speech is punctuated by the sound of shots from the glen where the family is being murdered.

Like Motes, the Misfit is fond of making absolute statements. As Motes insists that "blasphemy is the way to truth, . . . and there's no other way whether you understand it or not," so the Misfit says there is "no finer" woman than his mother and his father was "pure gold." His absolute statements only diminish when, talking about his doubt of Christ, they change into conditional sentences of an if/then pattern. Although the change in syntax does reflect his confusion, a rigid logical pattern is still maintained. "If He did what He said, then . . . throw away everything and follow Him . . . if He didn't, then . . . enjoy the few minutes you got left . . . if I had of been there, I would of known. . . ." (G, 28-29). The shots he fires, in effect, resolve the conditional sentences and end his doubts. His next words are an imperative, "Take her off and throw her where you thrown the others" (G, 29).

Images of burial or entrapment define every kind of human relation in O'Connor's incredibly hostile universe. It is not only social institutions, social workers, other people in general, and controlling parents in particular who can trap you; the very fact of growing up can do it. Images of entrapment often define adult life to a child. For example, as a boy, Hazel Motes talks his way into a tent for adults only at a country fair. Looking for his father, he finds instead a nude blonde woman lying in a velvet box. The tent seems an image for the adult world and the blonde in her coffin one for what he will find there: sex and death or, perhaps, death-inducing sex. In "A Temple of the Holy Ghost," the unnamed child heroine remembers an "adults only" tent decorated with stiff, painted figures who remind her of Christian martyrs. She daydreams about them trapped by Romans and waiting to have their tongues cut out. (A distinctively O'Connor association of martyrdom with silence.) Her image of Christians and Romans suggests the most prevalent relationship between people of all ages in O'Connor's fiction: oppressors and oppressed, murderers and victims.

The body is the worst of O'Connor's oppressors. It is a trap more profound than an unknown adult future or the power of Romans over Christians. Many of O'Connor's heroes are turned into psychic cripples by their bodies, or are literally buried alive in their own defective flesh. Never transcended or transformed by the spirit, the body often defines the self and expresses the form of the mind. In "Good Country People," Joy is not only forced to live with her mother in isolation because of her weak heart and artificial leg, she also seems compelled to define herself by them. Naming herself Hulga because it suits her body better than Joy, she names herself after her deformity, letting her artificial leg shape her identity. When the infamous Bible salesman steals it, he steals her essence, leaving her selfless among the red clay hills that loom around her like prison walls. Her deformity not only dictates her image of herself but also shapes her mother's view:

> She thought of her still as a child because it tore her heart to think instead of the poor stout girl in her thirties who had never danced a step or had any *normal* good times [G, 173].

Images of entrapment by the body frequently occur in connection with mechanical aids such as Hulga's artificial leg, Johnson's orthopedic shoe, Rayber's hearing aid, and dental braces worn by those innumerable ugly adolescent girls who populate O'Connor's South. Sorry and defective, the body must rely on steel and plastic to make it beautiful or even functional.

These devices are supposed to lessen and eliminate deformity, the overwhelming reality of O'Connor's heroes. Yet they either increase it or do nothing to diminish it. Hulga's leg in no way lessens her deformity, Rayber's hearing aid hears nothing essentially true. In the most significant moment of his life, the moment when he knows Bishop may scream if Tarwater tries to kill him, "he lay with his eyes closed as if listening to something he could hear only when his hearing aid was off. He sensed that he waited for a cataclysm." Similarly, Johnson refuses the orthopedic shoe that will reduce his limp and prefers to walk in pain, treating his foot "as if it were a sacred object." And none of those dental braces ever comes off.

In images of isolation and entrapment, O'Connor defines a world where life is a perpetual struggle, erupting in acts of violence, subsiding in an emotional void. In her earlier work, her themes evolve as a conflict between the present and the past variously expressed in social, religious, and psychological terms. Opposing images of rural and urban life express the social conflict while the religious one appears as a contrast between a sense of absolutes and damnation, and a secular, relativistic belief in human perfectibility. On a more philosophic plane, O'Connor offers an account of the mind/body problem in Milledgevillese and, psychologically, she describes the conflict between the past and present as a struggle between parent and child. Haze's double glance is frozen into a theme recurring throughout her work: the immobilization of a character before a present that is unfathomable—the leap through the window of a moving train, or a sense of his past felt in terms of disease, decay, suffering, and entrapment. While her sheer consistency of thought may seem irritating and mechanical, it cannot be attributed to banality of style or feeling.

O'Connor wrote about what she knew best: what it means to be a living contradiction. For her it meant an eternal cheeriness and loathing for life; graciousness and fear of human contact; acquiescence and enduring fury. Whether through some great effort of the will, or through some more mysterious and unconscious force, she created from that strife a powerful art, an art that was both a release and a vindication for her life. From the conflict she lived she created an uneasy alliance of the traditional and the modern where familiar Southern or Christian preoccupations explode in unexpected and unconventional directions.

If she set out to make morals, to praise the old values, she ended by engulfing all of them in an icy violence. If she began by mocking or damning her murderous heroes, she ended by exalting them. She grew to celebrate the liberating power of destruction. O'Connor became more and more the pure poet of the Misfit, the oppressed, the psychic cripple, the freak—of all of those who are martyred by silent fury and redeemed through violence.

2

Growing Up: Two Novels

In MOST NOVELS ABOUT GROWING UP, the hero encounters life like a flower blooming or a volcano erupting. In O'Connor's the hero's fear of life is so much greater than his longing for it that he continually avoids or protects himself from experience. In *Wise Blood* (1952) Hazel Motes wards off human contact with his religious obsession and his passion for objects. In *The Violent Bear It Away* (1960), young Tarwater's pervasive suspicion prevents him from getting too involved with Rayber. When their defenses eventually fall, both Motes and Tarwater flee from the terror of adult life by returning to the lives they knew as children. Motes's total disillusionment ends in his resuming the ritualistic suffering he practiced as a boy; Tarwater blots out his disturbing sexual encounter by resuming his childhood obedience to the old prophet. O'Connor's novels are, in a sense, about the impossibility of growing up, the destruction of hope, and the demolition of personality.

As O'Connor's heroes protect themselves from life, so O'Connor disengages herself from their constriction. In *Wise Blood* she both develops Motes's agony and mocks it. She not only afflicts him with a tendency to intellectualize, she herself treats him as a bodiless abstraction, a caricature of mind. Motes approaches life as a schoolboy approaches a problem in geometry. With grim determination, he allows his whole identity to depend on the verification of a number of opinions he holds in succession throughout the novel. The aphysical, intellectual quality of his search for life appears both in the rigidity of his thought and speech and in imagery of his flimsy physique. Haze's reasoning is concrete, but his body is ephemeral. "Haze's shadow was now behind him and now before him and now and then broken up by other people's shadows, but when it was by itself, stretching behind him, it was a thin nervous shadow walking backwards" (W, 37). His shadow, broken by the shadows of others and stretching away from his body, is a recurring image for his divided self. His self is so fragmented that it is always being absorbed by other selves. While Haze struggles to differentiate himself from others, he is always confronted by others who are not different from him. He finds his double everywhere. He is, at the same time, a replica of his grandfather, a double of Solace Layfield, whose consumptive cough he begins coughing after seeing him preach, and later the double of Asa Hawks, who is supposed to have blinded himself at a revival meeting as an act of faith.

As Hazel Motes becomes a parody of mind, so his disciple, Enoch Emory, is a caricature of body. Although he is earthy, interested in women, and concerned with acquiring a gorilla-like strength, his blood is wise blood, a bearer of intuitive knowledge, a form of intelligence. But all of this thinking, whether "logical" or intuitive, goes on in the face of total confusion. The novel is really an extended moment of indecision for Motes, an uncertainty captured in that powerful opening image when Haze looks out the window of the moving train, wanting to jump, and then looks back toward the end of the car at a Negro porter who claims to be from Chicago, the son of a railroad man, but who Haze is sure is the son of a Parrum "nigger who got the cholera from a pig." Haze looks at a present that is nothing but a blurry chaos and back at the physical origins of man doomed to share the fortunes and diseases of life with a pig. He is momentarily immobilized between the prospect of the window and the porter. His present and future are bound up in an indecipherable landscape that invites a leap into its nothingness; the past provides greater stability and the security of known and familiar things, but those things are always repulsive, always varieties of the most painful human experiences: disease, decay, and death.

Haze and even Enoch are both trying to think away chaos, to order and reduce the disorder embodied in that blurred landscape. Both are thinking out alternatives to a purely bestial, painful sense of life, a sense that demands you recognize your kinship to a diseased hog. But Motes's solutions only magnify the disorder. He argues against Christ and for blasphemy; against blasphemy and for total disbelief. After becoming an anti-Christ and an anti-anti-Christ, he reduces himself to total silence, a silence in which O'Connor eloquently destroys him.

Life refutes all of Motes's beliefs. The main line of O'Connor's complicated plot follows the progressive crushing of Motes's hopes and his ultimate "choice" of a life of physical pain. We first meet Motes on a train to Taulkinham,[1] a city where he hopes to prove that Christ did not exist. He begins his mission by visiting Mrs. Leora Watts, possessor of the friendliest bed in town, where he forces himself to lose his virginity to demonstrate that sin does not exist.

While walking the streets, he meets Asa Hawks and his daughter Sabbath, both street-corner evangelists. Hawks,

who turns out to be blind as a hawk, so fascinates Haze by
his total lack of concern for saving Haze's soul that Haze
follows him and decides to seduce his daughter to provoke
him. He has, however, trouble escaping her more authori-
tative advances. He meets Enoch Emory, who hears him
preach against Christ, who becomes his only disciple in the
Church without Christ, and who discovers a new Christ
for their church: a mummy lying in a glass case in the
"mvsuvm."[2]

Having failed to interest Hawks in his corruption, or
even to make Mrs. Watts believe that he is not a preacher
for Christ, Motes decides to change his image. He gets rid
of his black, "Jesus" hat, buys a bright new one and even a
car, a "rat-colored Essex" he comes to love. Equipped with
all the trappings of a man who knows there is no Christ and
no sin, Motes preaches his peculiar religion from the fender
of his car. He is approached by Hoover Shoats, a profes-
sional evangelist who wants to market Motes's ideas and go
into the anti-Christ business with him. Motes is too much
of an idealist to preach for Shoats and is outraged when he
finds that Shoats has hired Solace Layfield to dress in
clothes identical to his and to glorify his church, whose
name has grown to the "Holy Church of Christ Without
Christ." He runs over Solace for impersonating him.

When Enoch Emory, having successfully stolen the
mummy, brings it to his leader, Motes throws it against a
wall and destroys it. He decides to escape both Sabbath
and Enoch and to leave town to carry his "new" message
that blasphemy is futile, and that one should not believe in
anything. On the road, he is stopped by a policeman who,
learning that Motes has no driver's license, drives his beloved Essex off an embankment. Haze stares mutely at the
sky and walks back to town, quietly blinding himself with
lye when he gets to his boarding house. He begins sleeping

with three barbed wires around his chest and walking with broken glass in his shoes. He spends his days sitting in silence on the porch with his landlady, Mrs. Flood, who steals his money and eventually falls in love with him. To escape her offers of marriage, Motes leaves one morning only to be found in a ditch two days later by a couple of policemen who tell him to go back and pay his rent. They club him to death. The novel ends with Mrs. Flood staring intently into Motes's mutilated eye sockets, feeling very confused by it all.

What saves Motes from being no more than a burlesque of an anti-Christ or a parody of existential man is the very real pathos of his life. Haze's despair over Jesus has been explored at length by others,[3] but his more profound and more silent agony has been virtually ignored. Haze's most powerful feelings focus on objects or intellectual abstractions. His desire to leap through the window of the moving train, perhaps to escape the "Parrum nigger" whose father "got the cholera from a pig," could be narrowly seen as a desire for a leap into redeeming faith. But it seems to me that it is more a leap away from the natural world, away from the body, a leap toward becoming a thing.

Becoming a "thing" or a mechanical man is the only alternative O'Connor offers to the rather repulsive organic world. Alternating with images of bestial, decaying physical life, images of machines seem to describe a more orderly and enduring universe. Two worlds coexist in *Wise Blood:* one is a world of mechanical "becoming," a world that is like an elaborate erector set; the other is a world in decline and decay not unlike an open grave.

O'Connor's black sky is underpinned with silver streaks that look like scaffolding as though the universe were a city under construction (W, 37). O'Connor describes the cosmic process of becoming in terms of a universe of incorruptible metals. On a more human scale, Haze's rat-colored Essex expresses his own being, his desire to abstract himself from the human condition and become a thing in constant motion. The car is a mechanical extension of Motes, effective in killing Solace Layfield for being human enough to have a family to support and defective lungs. When it kills Solace, it kills what little bond Motes has with other men. It is only when it "dies," when the policeman drives it over an embankment, that Motes is totally crushed. The car has been his only connection to life, a pulpit that set him above other men and provided him with a clear relation to life as a denouncer of Jesus and a blasphemer. When it is destroyed he is overwhelmed by a sense of nothingness. By making his own eyes blind, he draws into himself the blankness of the sky. The organic, physical world he has tried to stave off with his abstractions and his religion of disbelief breaks upon him in affectless physical pain.

If Motes showed his distaste for the physical world by a desire to leap away from the porter whose origins are associated with sick swine, he shows his revulsion for the pleasures of animal life as well. He longs to leap again at the end of Chapter Two after he has come to Leora Watts to show that sin does not exist. Confronted with the physical reality of Leora, he wants to get away.[4] "If she had not held him so firmly by the arm, he might have leapt out the window" (W, 34). He stays with Mrs. Watts, who is very maternal but a "momma" who "don't mind if you ain't a preacher" (W, 34).

Whoever is not a preacher, not close to some system of abstractions, belongs to the other universe of the novel, the world of time and decay. Even the false preacher, the entrepreneur of evangelists, is called Hoover Shoats, a shoat or young pig. In fact, some of O'Connor's most ubiquitous characters are pigs. When Haze looks out the window of his Essex to see the world, he notices that:

> The sky leaked over all of it and then it began to leak into the car. The head of a string of pigs appeared snout-up over the ditch and he had to screech to a stop and watch the rear of the last pig disappear shaking into the ditch on the other side [W, 74].

Images of pigs and the "putty-colored" rain that falls on them define the visible world of most of O'Connor's heroes. Since they never see any more desirable landscape, the human face and body merge with the bestial world.

In the few instances where the body is not porcine, it is sinful. For example, Haze at ten seeks his father at a country fair in a tent marked "Sinsational." The "sin" he is most aware of seems to be that of having a body, for he assumes the tent contains something about two men in a privy. After associating sin with excretion, he thinks it might contain a man and a woman in a privy but, unable to dwell on the prospect, associates the forbidden tent with some violent act its white patrons are inflicting on a Negro. When he finally enters, he sees a nude blonde in a velvet box who he thinks is a skinned animal—not human at all. When he realizes she is a woman, he flees into his father's truck, fearing the response of his mother, whose "dresses are longer than other women's" and who knows, after one look at him, that he has sinned.

Although Motes resents his mother, he is like her. After she beats him he begins to punish himself, filling his shoes with pebbles and walking through the woods. That he has adopted his mother's view of the world is further suggested in his taking with him only one book when he went into the army, the Bible, which he "didn't read . . . often but

when he did he wore his mother's glasses" (W, 23), although his own vision is not weak. Lying in his berth in the
opening chapter, he dreams about his mother in her coffin
and as he remembers her face, as dissatisfied in death as it
was in life, he cannot distinguish himself in his berth from
her in her coffin. In his dream she looks

> as if she were going to spring up and shove the lid back and
> fly out and satisfy herself. . . . She might have been going
> to spring. He saw her in his sleep, terrible, like a huge bat,
> dart from the closing, fly out of there [W, 2].

Waking up terrified in his berth, he calls for the porter,
Parrum, to release him. Parrum, the aforementioned son of
a Negro who died from a pig's cholera, seems to be an embodiment of mortality. Even his name is suggestive of
birth. And Haze trapped in his berth/birth calls for release
from his mother. The fact that the porter—carrier or de-
liverer—is a man may suggest that it is in the male world of
action that he sought safety. But his father, who did not
seem guilty about watching the boxed blonde, did not free
him. Nor did his preacher grandfather, from whom he
learned of Jesus as a principle of death, destruction, and decay. For Motes, Jesus is a figure swinging like an ape in the
back of his mind, a culmination of the animal world repre-
senting a kind of quintessential mortality.

Although neither his father nor grandfather could free
him from looking at the world through his mother's eyes,
he is freed by the Parrum porter, who ushers him into the
scene of his most active life, Taulkinham. He has tried unsuccessfully "to stay in Eastrod with his two eyes open,
and his hands always handling the familiar thing, his feet
on the known track and his tongue not too loose" (W, 16).
In both his old and new attempts to avoid Jesus (sin, decay,

death) he denies he has a body and hopes to avoid his mortality by looking to the outer world, a world that hovers between abstract thought and tangible, concrete things.[5]

Since he cannot see his own body or the bodies of women apart from sin and hell, he seizes on objects to anchor him to the tangible, visible world. He feels his resemblance to a preacher will be eliminated because of his new white hat, and his car—the rat-colored Essex that links him to the wider social world. That the car comes to stand for the human condition of Hazel Motes is clear in one of Haze's dreams and his self-blinding at the close of the book.

Haze's dream is, in part, about Enoch Emory, his more homey counterpart. Wounded by Haze in front of the museum, Enoch sees his blood on the ground as a spring of wise blood, of intuitive knowledge in the heart of the city. His blood leads him to the mummy, the new Jesus shrunk to three feet by "A-rabs," who appears in two important scenes which may occur simultaneously. While Enoch steals the mummy and brings him home to rest in his gilded commode, Motes sleeps in his rat-colored Essex, dreaming the dream of the theft. The mummy, who Enoch says had "never done anything but get himself embalmed and then lain stinking in a museum the rest of his life" (W, 176), is not exactly dead. Similarly, Motes dreams of himself that "he was not exactly dead but only buried."

> He was not waiting on the Judgment because there was no Judgment, he was waiting on nothing. Various eyes looked through the back oval window at his situation, some with considerable reverence, like the boy from the zoo, and some only to see what they could see. There were three women with paper sacks who looked at him critically as if he were something—a piece of fish—they might buy, but they passed on after a minute. A man in a canvas hat looked in and put his thumb to his nose and wiggled his fingers. Then

a woman with two little boys on either side of her stopped and looked in, grinning. After a second, she pushed the boys out of view and indicated that she would climb in and keep them company for a while, but she couldn't get through the glass and finally she went off. All this time Haze was bent on getting out but since there was no use to try, he didn't make any move one way or the other. He kept expecting Hawks to appear at the oval window with a wrench, but the blind man didn't come [W, 160-161].

Like the mummy in his case, Haze in his car is on display to whoever passes. In his dream he seems visited by most of the characters in the novel. Enoch regards him with a reverence as great as he shows the mummy, the three women who pass may be the three women of the novel: Leora Watts, Sabbath Hawks, and his mother, who all size him up sexually. The woman with her sons who wants to climb in with him may be the swimmer from the park's pool whose strapless bathing suit seemed so daring to Enoch and Haze; or she may be Sabbath Hawks, who is eager for a sexual involvement with him but whom he wards off as best he can. The man in the canvas hat who mocks him may be any of the derisive males in the book— from his father to Onnie Jay to Jesus himself—who have managed not to be trapped in a shell or buried in a glass coffin. He may be Asa Hawks, whom Haze relies on to save him from his mortality by converting him to Christ. Like Haze's first dream, which ended in his calling for Parrum, Haze calls again for some absent male to come and release him from entrapment and bondage. Both the mummy and Motes dreaming of himself as mummy become images of the human condition: life is not exactly death but is waiting for nothing.

When Enoch brings Haze the mummy, Sabbath sees it as a quintessence of everyone she has ever known, recognizing it as an image of mortality. Motes throws it against the wall, cracking its skull. The destruction of the mummy, and the murder of Solace Layfield, may be gestures toward suicide. Motes has tried to protect himself from Jesus with his mind, by reasoning what the effect of Jesus would be if He had existed. He breaks the head of the mummy, a head full of trash that sprays out in dust. In splitting the mummy's skull, Motes expresses his own self-hatred and attempts to kill both his own mortality, his own physical being, and the need for abstractions in himself. After claiming to be, in effect, the new Jesus, he kills the symbol of the new Jesus. After destroying the mummy, he does destroy his own reliance on abstractions. He affirms that "it was not right to believe anything you couldn't see or hold in your hands or test with your teeth" (W, 206). He no longer believes that blasphemy is the only way to truth because even that "meant you were believing in something to blaspheme" (W, 206).

After concluding that all you can know is what you see, Haze moves from the phenomenological to the existential. When the policeman destroys his beloved Essex by pushing it down an embankment, Motes sees nothingness for the first time. He has a vision that "extended from his eyes to the blank gray sky that went on, depth after depth into space" (W, 209). He explains to Mrs. Flood that he has blinded himself because "blind eyes can hold more." It seems likely that what they hold more of is nothingness. After losing his car, his bond with the physical world, he has nothing at all. His shock at seeing the abyss, perhaps imaged as the embankment the car falls over, passes into a desire for another anchor. He has gone from believing in but avoiding Jesus as a child, to preaching disbelief in Jesus, to propounding what is: from fear to blasphemy to a phenomenology in which all he can know is what he can see.

After losing his Essex, he is engulfed in a sense of nothingness, a mental emptiness broken by ambiguous, irrelevant symbols.

Motes begins to keep stones and glass in his shoes; he binds three strands of barbed wire around his chest and remains silent most of the day. The glass and wire anchor him to life and produce an animal pain that is the only sensation he can accept. When Mrs. Flood, mystified by his ritualistic suffering, asks him the reason for it, Motes claims that he is "paying" but refuses to explain what he is paying for. What he is paying for is ambiguous. He chooses to pay as he paid for disobeying his mother's sexual prohibitions as a child. Mrs. Flood is so hurt by his not loving her that she punishes him for obeying them. After he leaves her, she calls the police and claims Motes has gone off without paying his rent. Perhaps Motes is paying the price of having a body that can do nothing but suffer whether it has been titillated, loved, or mortified.[6]

Motes could, after the death of the Essex, have seen heaven, his own self, or even an anti-self, a believer or a blasphemer or a scientist, which is, to O'Connor, a chronicler of what is. But what he sees is blankness, a nothingness that engulfs him after the gratuitous destruction of his rat-colored car, the instrument of his life and mobility. All the novel's gratuitous acts of violence: the self-inflicted punishment at ten, the murder of Solace Layfield, the destruction of the mummy, the rejection of Enoch Emory, and the demise of the Essex, culminate in Haze's enigmatic self-blinding and castigation.

The ambiguity of the ending makes it possible to believe that what Motes sees in the blank sky is less than total blankness—that he sees the vanity of his pretensions and is mortifying himself to atone for his disbelief. This is a simplistic view that can best be maintained by readers with dogmatic glasses. It is, I feel, their glasses and not the text that suggest this. Haze maintains until the end the non-existence of Jesus. Since pain is the only attribute of life for him, perhaps he tortures himself to assert his own existence. His suffering is both proof that he has survived, and the price he pays for being alive. By clinging to silence, broken glass and barbed wire, Motes affirms himself and embraces his pain as the sign of his own life.

The novel concludes with Mrs. Flood, who, like the original flood, engulfs everything mortal. It is, in a sense, her love and tenderness that overwhelm Motes and frighten him away. And it is her passion for his return that makes her call the police. Over and over again in O'Connor's world, human tenderness kills.

Mrs. Flood "was not a woman who felt more violence in one word than in another: she took every word at its face value but all the faces were the same" (W, 114). Motes, with his scarred face, his peculiar silence, is different. The point of light he becomes for her has its source in what is most different about him—his scarred and mutilated eye sockets. That point of light receding into the distance, unknown yet profoundly familiar, Mrs. Flood sees with her eyes shut. Merging with her image of Haze's shattered, wounded body, the light may be no more than the glow of decomposing tissue, the light of mortality.

Like *Wise Blood*, O'Connor's second novel, *The Violent Bear It Away*, is a novel of initiation.[7] It opens with Francis Marion Tarwater, son of a divinity student and a young unmarried woman, burying the great-uncle who raised him. Mason Tarwater kidnaped him from his uncle Rayber, a schoolteacher who wanted to raise him according to the latest psychology of child-rearing and the principles of reason. Instead, the boy grew up with the old prophet in Powderhead, an isolated backwoods farm, in the company of some Negro neighbors, Daniel, Ezekiel, and Noah. Raised to be a prophet like his great-uncle, the boy has been given two missions: to bury the old man when he dies, and to baptize Bishop, the idiot son of Rayber and a middle-aged "welfare-woman" who deserted Rayber when he refused to institutionalize the child.

As the boy digs Mason's grave, he hears a strange voice disparaging the prophet and encouraging him to do all the things he forbade: to drink, to seek the company of Rayber, and to doubt his mission.[8] After drinking some corn liquor from his great-uncle's still, he falls into a drunken sleep. When he wakes, he sets fire to the house, where he thinks his uncle still sits dead at the breakfast table, and hitch-hikes to the city to Rayber, whom the old prophet had kidnaped in his youth and tried, unsuccessfully, to convert. A copper-flue salesman drives him into town and helps him telephone Rayber. When Bishop answers, gurgling into the phone, he reacts violently against him, slams down the phone and sets out to find Rayber's house.

Rayber greets him as the son he has always wanted, the boy he could have sent to college. Rayber shows him the city, introduces him to new ideas, and makes every attempt to get through to him. Although the boy has a grudging admiration for Rayber, he is unable to admit it to himself or his uncle. The main action of the novel, Rayber's attempts to interest the boy in a larger social reality and to reach him in a personal way, evolves into an extended moment of indecision for the boy. As Motes was paralyzed between the window and the porter, so he is immobilized between the vague, unreal future Rayber offers him and the life created for him by the old prophet. He decides that he has to prove he is not a prophet by becoming a murderer; he kills Bishop to demonstrate his freedom from the old man and, by performing an act Rayber attempted without success, to prove his superiority to his uncle.

After drowning Bishop, he hitch-hikes toward home with a truck driver. He tries to buy a cold drink from a woman who ran a grocery near Powderhead and knew his uncle. Having heard of his failure to bury old Tarwater, she refuses to serve him, and rebukes him for setting fire to the house. Involuntarily shouting an obscenity at her, he moves down the road to hitch a ride home. He is picked up by a homosexual driving a lavender and cream car, who offers him marijuana and whiskey.[9] When the boy passes out, the homosexual turns off the road, rapes the boy, and steals the bottle opener and corkscrew Rayber gave him. Feeling defiled when he wakes, the boy sets fire to the grove where he has been used and abandoned and goes toward his uncle's grave. Lying on it, pressing his face to it, he hears the command, whose words, "GO WARN THE CHIL-DREN OF GOD OF THE TERRIBLE SPEED OF MERCY," are as silent as seeds opening one at a time in his blood" (V, 242). Smearing his forehead with earth from old Tarwater's grave, he moves toward the city to obey the command.

That conflict is the main theme of the novel is suggested by the name of the prophet that dominates it, Tarwater, an embodiment of things that do not mix. Tarwater, in effect, fights with Rayber for possession of the boy who is both Rayber and Tarwater (Rayber is his legal name as the child of his uncle's unmarried sister, Tarwater the name the old prophet has raised him with). Reflecting the theme of conflict, the structure of the novel depends heavily on two of O'Connor's favorite devices: the use of warring doubles and the repetition of the same struggle. Old Tarwater's adventures span three generations. He has tried to save his sister, his sister's son, and his sister's grandson in succession.

He identifies himself with the patriarchs Jonah, Ezekiel, and Daniel and claims to have saved his grand-nephew from a schoolroom run by women and given him the more desirable companionship of Abel, Enoch, Noah, Job, Abraham, King David, and Solomon. He raises the boy without women or any knowledge of them other than that they are all whores except for Bernice Bishop, the welfare woman, who was too ridiculous even to achieve that status. Through the old prophet's eyes, the boy sees all of reality, all of history from Adam's expulsion from the garden through the presidency of Herbert Hoover to the Second Coming and the Day of Judgment.[10]

The boy walks through the world looking for symbols, signs that he has been called and that God has a destiny for him greater than the mission his great-uncle gave him: the baptism of an idiot child. He is immobilized for the extended moment of the novel between the real world of corn liquor, psychological tests, school, the city park, and the possibility that any or all of these may not be real but symbolic, that the sunlight shining on Bishop's head as he jumps into a fountain in the park may be the finger of God pointing out Bishop for baptism.

The values of Rayber and Tarwater polarize into literal and symbolic views of reality, secular and religious views of life. The two men represent mutually estranged realities which can only meet in common gestures of violence or, as Le Clézio would have it, in their mutual desire to engulf the boy, to use him as a tool to destroy *"le néant."* Although they are estranged from each other, they cannot survive alone but are unwillingly joined in an endless struggle, forced to recognize some essential kinship.

Their connection with each other is objectified in the novel by the use of doubles. For example, Bishop is the double of the old prophet, reflecting both his innocence and his idiocy. The stranger who speaks to young Tarwater as he buries the old prophet is an aspect of himself: "He began to feel that he was only just now meeting himself, as if as long as his uncle had lived, he had been deprived of his own acquaintance" (V, 35). The child, Bishop, who looks like the prophet, is also compared to the deformed part of Rayber, joined to him as his hearing aid is joined to his ear. Because of this, the child may represent Rayber's relation to the prophet who kidnaped him in his own childhood. He is, in fact, deaf because of old Tarwater, who shot him in the ear when he tried to "rescue" the boy. Rayber's enduring rage at the old prophet appears obliquely when, after following the boy to a revival meeting, he sees a beautiful, crippled child who is, along with her parents, an evangelist. He sees her belief in both God and her parents as the curse on the young, the trusting, and the hopeful. Embodying Rayber's feelings about himself and his nephew, the girl becomes a quintessential, ignorant victim of all the fierce old prophets who extract belief as the price of life.

Longing to destroy all the old Tarwater within the boy, Rayber drowns the boy's clothes. When the boy drowns Bishop, who looks exactly like the old prophet, the boy tries to free himself. He murders to kill his attachment to the old man and to end the childhood in which the old prophet has held him. All he does achieve is a perverse sexual growth. He shouts an obscenity at the grocery woman who knew his great-uncle when she refuses him a purple drink. It is the first he with his "immense contempt for the flesh" has ever spoken. The homosexual who gives him a ride in his "lavender and cream" car offers him marijuana and whiskey, and initiates him into one kind of sexuality[11] that may also suggest an aspect of the boy's self. Like those all-too-familiar strangers O'Connor's heroes always encounter, he may be the boy's future double.

Young Tarwater recoils in terror from what he has unleashed in the present and what the future may hold in
store. He reverts immediately to his great-uncle and tries to
escape the self he has become by returning to what he has
been. Making an attempt to flee the self that has been used
and dirtied, he returns to the self his uncle created for him,
a self inextricable from the old man.

The Violent Bear It Away begins and ends with an encounter with a stranger, each an aspect of young Tarwater's being: the strange voice encouraging him to seek
Rayber, and the homosexual male who may suggest the
boy's future. The rejection of both strangers, the rubbing
of his forehead with soil from the old man's grave, signal
the boy's rejection of his own identity and his final burial.
He covers himself with his great-uncle's clay, disappearing
within his shell. That homosexual who took away Rayber's
gifts, the corkscrew and bottle opener that might have
opened the wine of life, took away the boy's sexuality and
maturity.[12]

Life makes O'Connor's heroes crumble. Both *Wise
Blood* and *The Violent Bear It Away* explore the long moment of fear in which, after years of resentful obedience,
they discover they must choose their life. Yet both are incapable of making a choice. No matter what Motes does he
can never stop looking at the world through his mother's
glasses; nor can young Tarwater see very far beyond the
old prophet's suspicion. Although O'Connor mocks Motes
and exalts Tarwater, she gives them a similar fate. Their
sheer inability to tolerate complexity, ambivalence, and
human passion, and their overwhelming rigidity, force
them to run from whatever alternatives life presents, to
abdicate adulthood in favor of their old familiar pain. Both
Motes and Tarwater are, in a sense, freed from adult com-
plexities by their ability to play out a childhood role for a

lifetime. The role may be painful, but it is safe and secure. In traditional terms, neither hero "grows up." Tarwater becomes a replica of the prophet and Motes turns into a logical absurdity: a suffering mechanical man.

These novels of initiation are, to an astonishing extent, about the impossibility of staying initiated. O'Connor's accounts of growing up are about the impossibility of either growth or adult life. While O'Connor never achieved in either novel the power and force she could bring to the short story, they remain remarkable renderings of youths cursed by self-loathing who learn, at a very early age, the Misfit's lesson: "There's no real pleasure in life." Motes and Tarwater suffer from ice in the blood, from a pervasive emotional exhaustion broken only by episodic violence. O'Connor never treats growing up as a smooth continuum; she sees it as a crisis or, more accurately, as a long and directionless repetition of the same crisis. Over and over her heroes try to disengage themselves from their "parents" and from all human ties. In the degree to which their growth occurs externally and mechanically as a series of increasingly violent acts, O'Connor may have created, in her peculiar backwoods heroes, heroes of our time. They rise to violence only to fall back into exhaustion and passivity. Or they exalt their obedience as a paradoxical sign of their power. But they never melt the ice in their blood, that essential emotional death that preserves them in their passive, lonely fury.

3

Living in the World:

People & Things in

A GOOD MAN IS HARD TO FIND

THE STORIES OF *A Good Man Is Hard to Find* (1955) all
develop themes O'Connor introduced in *Wise Blood*
(1952). While everyone in the collection may be looking
for his own particular Jesus, that good man who is so very
hard to find, few of them do more than stumble over the innumerable hogs that populate O'Connor's South. The stories of the collection may be close-ups of what Haze sees
from his train window and at the back of the car: nothingness and the kinship of men and swine. The heroes of the
book waver between a sense of vacancy and nothingness
and disgust at their own bodies and even the natural world.

Conflict appears in the collection as the duality of matter
and spirit, the body and the mind. Although many an
American writer before her has been preoccupied with this
peculiar, almost Manichean, duality, O'Connor's conception and resolution of the problem are unique. The stories
I will discuss, "The Life You Save May Be Your Own,"
"Good Country People," and "A Temple of the Holy
Ghost," are three major variations on O'Connor's essential
theme.

The first describes the gap between physical and spiritual life or, in other words, the incommensurability of

facts and essences. The second is about the effect of things, objects, or machines on the mind or, in other words, the relation of the material to the mental. The third story reverses the emphasis of the first and describes the effect of spiritual life on physical life. All of these stories are about the relation—whether of closeness or distance—of the mind and body. O'Connor consistently opposes the spiritual and physical, keeping them so separate and dual that no one seems to have both a mind and body at the same time. Never mingling or reaching equilibrium, they seem, like Rayber and the old prophet, locked in an endless struggle for supremacy. The alternation appears in style as an uneasy wavering between symbolism, allegory, and literal description. This is especially clear in "The Life You Save May Be Your Own."

Embedded in O'Connor's tale of cruelty is a recurring sense of the mind in conflict with the whole of the physical world. Like most of O'Connor's stories, "The Life You Save May Be Your Own" has an inconsequential plot. A one-armed tramp comes to the farm of Mrs. Lucynell Crater and her deaf, thirtyish daughter, Lucynell, who has never learned to speak. He calls himself Tom T. Shiftlet, a carpenter and a man possessing a "moral intelligence," a man more concerned with spiritual than material wealth. Mrs. Crater, eager for a son-in-law, offers him Lucynell, her farm, a car, and, when pressed, agrees to throw in seventeen dollars for a honeymoon. He marries Lucynell and drives off with her. While stopping at a diner, Lucynell falls asleep and Shiftlet leaves her there, telling the counterman that she is a hitch-hiker. Driving toward Mobile, he picks up a hitch-hiking boy as he feels his responsibility as a car owner requires.[1]

The story is a good example of the tendency of O'Connor's real portraits to overpower her allegorical ones. That

to travel from place to place

she obviously hoped to give symbolic overtones to the story is suggested by Shiftlet's figure forming a crooked cross against the sky, his occupation as an itinerant carpenter, his assertion that the spirit is more important than the body, his teaching Lucynell what might be a Holy Ghost reference, the word "bird," and his association with sun and light imagery. What emerges most powerfully in the story is more literal: a landscape of a withered universe reduced to the size of a small farm, bounded by three mountains and a chicken coop. Everyone in it is in some way warped or deformed; its air is thick and so dusty that clouds grow in it like turnips.

The owner of the world is Mrs. Crater, whose name suggests the abyss in a dwarfed universe. The abyss is sheer mortality, the inescapable crater of the grave. Mrs. Crater is associated with time and decay, with the whole of the organic world in decline. She is not a cedar, symbol of wealth and prosperity, but is "the size of a cedar fence post," a durable bit of weathered wood. When she reminds Shiftlet of his physical being, calling him a homeless, disabled drifter, "the ugly words settled in Mr. Shiftlet's head like a group of buzzards on top of a tree." These are the vultures of Shiftlet's mind, birds that remind him of his mortality.

Denying the relevance of the body, Shiftlet greets Lucynell as though she were not afflicted, offers Mrs. Crater chewing gum although she has no teeth, and ignores his own problem. His own body emerges slowly from the road through bright sunlight that first screens it and then turns it into a silhouette of a crooked cross until he comes near, when he looks like "a bird that had come up very close." After Lucynell thinks of him as a bird, he spots the old automobile. The bird and car are images for Shiftlet, who is always associated with motion, speed, and detach-

ment. When he learns the car stopped running when Mr.
Crater died, he comments on the mystery of life, the
enigma of the heart and, perhaps, of love. He tells about an
Atlanta doctor who cut out a human heart and held it in
his hand "and studied it like it was a day-old chicken, and
lady, . . . he don't know more about it than you or me"
(G, 55).

The dissection of the heart in Atlanta is the first of four
dissections in the story. Shiftlet tries to probe the mystery
of flame, lighting a match and staring at it until it seems
about to burn his fingers and nose. Unable to solve the
enigma of flame, he begins to anatomize himself into the
possible selves he contains. He demands of Mrs. Crater

> How you know my name ain't Aaron Sparks, lady, and I
> come from Singleberry, Georgia, or how you know it's
> not George Speeds and I come from Lucy, Alabama, or
> how you know I ain't Thompson Bright from Toolafalls,
> Mississippi? [G, 56]

Shiftlet may be all of these. Like Aaron, his embodiment of
spirit, his god, is an object—not a golden calf but an automobile. Sparks and Bright suggest fire and light, with
which he is associated in imagery. Speeds, like his association with birds, drifting, and motion defines what he thinks
of as spirit: constant motion. All of these names suit him as
well as Shiftlet.

For Mrs. Crater, a man is what he does—what tools he
carries in his box. When she tells him she cannot pay for
his carpentry, he says that some things mean more to him
than money. Yet, in imagery, when he says this he suggests
the opposite. Lucynell watches the "trigger that moved up
and down in his neck" hearing words spoken like bullets,
denials of the material world. Yet his life is remarkably literal. He has been in the "Arm Service" and lost a service-

able arm. While he insists the world seems whole only in desolate country where he can see the sunset, his eyes keep returning to the automobile gleaming in the dark. When Mrs. Crater offers it to him as a house, Shiftlet likens it to the coffins monks sleep in. As death is to the monks, so the car is to him, a way of life. Like his ancestor Hazel Motes, he likes living in a car. It gives him a place to "be" while he thinks of moving around.

On Mrs. Crater's farm, O'Connor's microcosmic universe, Shiftlet repairs the fence and steps, and works up to his most spectacular feat, the resurrection of the car. Like the Atlanta doctor, he cuts up its insides after he "raised the hood and studied its mechanism" (G, 60). He repairs it by a kind of inspiration, a mechanical afflatus: a fan belt. As the car begins to move, Mrs. Crater begins pushing Lucynell, who yells "burrddttt!" over and over. The life Shiftlet saves is not his own but is the life of his ideal self-image, the car.

When Mrs. Crater explicitly tells him to marry Lucynell, and reminds him she is offering a home to a lone, disabled man, he answers

> Lady, a man is divided into two parts, body and spirit. . . .
> The body, lady, is like a house: it don't go anywhere; but
> the spirit, lady, is like a automobile, always on the move,
> always. . . . [G, 63].

When Mrs. Crater reminds him of the comforts of her home, agrees to let him paint the car, and gives him money for his honeymoon, she figuratively gilds his calf, his idol. The similitude between the car and spirit disappears into metaphor: the car *is* spirit or motion.

Nothing but paper work and blood tests, Shiftlet's marriage is too physical for him. Leaving Mrs. Crater at her farm, he drives as fast as he can toward Mobile. He abandons Lucynell without malice or pleasure, leaving her in the Hot Spot at a time when things are getting hot for him, when his fantasy of himself as a good man is about to be threatened as his detachment is threatened by the presence of a woman for the night. Perhaps he fears that "sly isolated little thought like a shoot of green in the desert" (G, 65) that changes Lucynell's placid expression.

After he abandons Lucynell, the feelings he cannot demonstrate are objectified in a real encounter and in the description O'Connor provides of the real world. The story becomes a projection of his emotional state. His perception of the world gradually changes, becoming more childlike. He sees that "deep in the sky a storm was preparing very slowly and without thunder as if it meant to drain every drop of air from the earth before it broke" (G, 66). The storm suggests Shiftlet's quiet, affectless cruelty as much as it prepares for the rainfall to come. The sun, first appearing in the story as shapeless light, then as a sphere balanced on a mountain, then as a visitor of the chicken coop, is now a ball, a child's toy. It rolls toward him "directly in front of the automobile. It was a reddening ball that through his windshield was slightly flat on the bottom and top" (G, 66). After seeing the sun as a ball, he sees a boy who he knows intuitively is a hitch-hiker and whose "hat was set on his head in a way to indicate that he had left somewhere for good" (G, 66).

His encounter with the boy offers an objective recapitulation of his own abandonment of the security of Mrs. Crater's farm and, as we learn, of his own abandonment of his mother. Like Lucynell, his mother was an "angel of Gawd" whom he deserted. He has persistently denied the significance of the heart (love) and the blood (kinship).

Yet he was deeply hurt by the word "milk" when Mrs. Crater told him not to try to milk her any more. While denying the value of what she gives, he cannot stop himself from taking it. Perhaps he is so pained by Mrs. Crater's unwillingness to be milked because he needs as much mother's milk as he can get. While running away from his wife and mother-in-law Shiftlet meets himself running away from home as a child.

His loathing of his own body is so great that he can love only a machine, a car that can carry a woman who is an "angel of Gawd" but permits him to run away before she becomes a sexual being. By seeing his wife and mother as angels who cannot and should not be touched, he evades his own sexual fear, justifying it as a sign of his moral sense and spiritual bias.

Instead of escaping from his body, from a sense of organic decay, he is literally drowning in mud. Through thick and suffocating air lit dimly by a sun like a child's toy, the boy calls his own mother a stinking polecat and Shiftlet's a fleabag. Shiftlet feels the rottenness of the world lies in its physicality—in both its vegetable and animal life. He resents that even clouds can be the color of a boy's hat, that some human element can put the lid on him and the world, and that he is cosmically confined in his own mortality. As the turnip-cloud descends he appeals to God to help him, to "break forth and wash the slime from this earth!" (G, 68). He is answered not by a human God but by a kind of eternal machine that guffaws, explodes in thunder, and lets a shower of metal fall. "Fantastic raindrops, like tin-can tops, crashed over the rear of Mr. Shiftlet's car" (G, 68). Shiftlet is restored. He sticks his stump out the window of the car, touching the only substance he can touch: rain like tin, rain like part of the metallic world. Racing toward Mobile, the only city in the state looking out on the open sea, he drives toward motion unlimited by clay.

The "Good Country People" O'Connor writes about are very much like the folks on Mrs. Crater's farm. Mrs. Crater is there herself, her character divided between Mrs. Freeman, who is obsessed with disease, decay, and the aberrations of the organic, and Mrs. Hopewell, a controlling but well-intentioned mother who, with a desperate optimism, refuses to see the grotesque. Lucynell Crater appears as Joy Hopewell, a thirtyish, afflicted woman who tries to pass herself off as a teenager. Like Shiftlet, Manley Pointer is a drifting man claiming a moral intelligence. As "The Life You Save May Be Your Own" developed the conflict of the mind with the body, the spiritual with the material world, so "Good Country People" explores another relation of people to things, that of the self to the world around it.

The story opens with a description of Mrs. Freeman, hired help of Mrs. Hopewell, who, having divorced her husband years ago, runs her farm alone. She has hired Mrs. Freeman and her husband because they are good country people and no one else wanted the job. Mrs. Hopewell lives with her daughter, Joy, an atheist, intellectual, and Ph.D. in philosophy who has a weak heart and a wooden leg and who, at twenty-one when she was away from home, changed her name to Hulga. A Bible salesman named Manley Pointer calls on them and tries to sell Mrs. Hopewell a Bible. Although she does not buy his Bible, she feels compassion for him when, telling her of his weak heart, he reminds her of Joy's illness. Impulsively, Mrs. Hopewell asks him to stay for dinner. When he leaves, Hulga walks him to the front gate and they arrange to meet the following day for a picnic. Her evening is spent in fantasies of seducing him. Yet the following day, after they talk, and kiss, and Hulga lets him remove her artificial leg, he merely steals the leg and runs off through the fields. The story ends with Mrs. Freeman smelling an evil-smelling onion shoot, reflecting that she could never be simple enough to be religious.[2]

Mrs. Freeman, whose "forward expression was steady and driving like the advance of a heavy truck" (G, 169), is associated with machines—most often with those metallic defenses against lingering and incurable disease. Her own progress through experience is channeled by road signs, by yellow lines down the center of an episode. Her daughters, Glynese and Carramae, with their vomit and sties, are too visceral for Joy-Hulga, who calls them Glycerin and Cara-mel, those sticky substances which, she feels, define them. Joy-Hulga has turned from the physical world, where her eyes see through to nothing, to a world of abstractions. Her contempt for the natural world is so great that she has tried to blot it out. Her

> constant outrage had obliterated every expression from her face, [she] would stare just a little to the side of her, her eyes icy blue, with the look of someone who has achieved blindness by an act of will and means to keep it. [G, 171]

The world Joy-Hulga wants to shut out is the farm life of her mother, filled with her mother's desperate attempts to ignore or minimize her deformity and filled with the clichés that define the range of Mrs. Hopewell's feeling. Mrs. Hopewell can reduce anything to one of her favorite remarks: "Nothing is perfect. This was one of Mrs. Hopewell's favorite sayings. Another was: that is life! And still another, the most important, was: well, other people have their opinions too" (G, 171). Mrs. Hopewell, recognizing Mrs. Freeman's affinity for inexorable machines, calls her the creator of her husband's fate, "the wheel behind the wheel." Their dialogue is one of the great achievements of O'Connor's style. Mrs. Freeman begins:

> "It's some that are quicker than others."
> "Everybody is different," Mrs. Hopewell said.
> "Yes, most people is," Mrs. Freeman said.
> "It takes all kinds to make the world."
> "I always said it did myself." [G, 172].

As Mrs. Hopewell reduces the dimensions of human difference, so she reduces the size of her daughter, preferring to think of her as a child rather than a grown woman who has had a weak heart and wooden leg for twenty years. She calls Hulga Joy, the name of her childhood.

Joy-Hulga has willed herself to blindness to the awful face of Mrs. Freeman, whose glance is still more terribly fixed on the aberrant and grotesque. She searches the newspapers daily for stories of odd diseases and unusual events, her recent favorite being the tale of a woman who conceived and gave birth in an iron lung. For the vomiting of Mrs. Freeman's pregnant daughter, and the sty of her single one, Hulga has infinite contempt, equaled only by her feeling for trees, fields, flowers, and men. Having willed herself to blindness to the physical world, she turns her vision toward abstraction. Her motive and point of view are revealed explicitly in the story by her comment to her mother and her underlinings in a book about science. She quotes Malebranche to Mrs. Hopewell, crying, "Malebranche was right: we are not our own light. We are not our own light" (G, 176). While she accuses her mother of not seeing how banal she is, it is Hulga who does not want to see herself. Having named herself after her deformity, she nevertheless rarely looks at it directly.

The screen of abstractions she has built between herself, her body, and the world is as much an expression of her longing for them as a sign of her blindness. Deformed and feeble himself, Malebranche, like Hulga, preached the dualism of mind and body, claiming that there was no interaction between them or, in effect, that the body had no power over the mind. Yet Hulga's maimed body has formed her mind, shaped her identity, and turned her life into a reaction against her own body. She shows her contempt for herself and her mother by "becoming less like other people and more like herself—bloated, rude, and squint-eyed" (G, 176). She shows her desire not to see herself by escaping into a philosophy or fantasy. Her blindness is a kind of emotional death, an inability to feel anything but contempt for life. She is able to see things only as though they were at a great distance, phenomena to be studied through a telescope. She can accept that science wants "to know nothing of nothing" (G, 178). Like her more spectacular counterpart Hazel Motes, she combines a need for abstractions with a fondness for things.

The supreme act of Hulga's life is the creation of her own self—the renaming of herself in the shape of her deformity and weakness. She called herself Hulga when "she had a vision of the name working like the ugly sweating Vulcan who stayed in the furnace and to whom, presumably, the goddess had to come when called (G, 174). Changing her name, ridiculing Mrs. Freeman, becoming bloated, and wearing an absurd shirt with a cowboy on it seem to be ways of attacking Mrs. Hopewell. "One of her major triumphs was that her mother had not been able to turn her dust into Joy, but the greater one was that she had been able to turn it herself into Hulga" (G, 174).

Joy-Hulga sees her body as dust, as a mass of particles that could have been shaped by her mother into Joy but that she turned into Hulga, a mimic Vulcan playing the part of unavoidable ugliness, death and decay—the inescapable end of beauty. For her mother, she becomes a symbol of everything Mrs. Hopewell wants to deny. When Manley Pointer enters and calls her Mrs. Cedars, the name of her farm, he calls her by the scriptural tree symbolizing power, prosperity, and longevity. He calls her by the name of her self-image.

The scenes between Pointer and Hulga define the relation of the body to the mind, the intellectual and emotional life. Hulga, the philosopher, claims she can see through to nothing, does not believe in God, and lives a life without illusions yet finds herself wearing Vapex on her collar and claiming to be seventeen. Amused that he brought his Bible case on their foodless picnic, she finds herself unaffected by his kisses. "Even before he released her, her mind, clear and detached and ironic anyway, was regarding him from a great distance with amusement but with pity" (G, 188).

When they walk through the fields into the barn, Manley takes her glasses and, when he demands to be told she loves him, hears instead that she can see through to nothing. Her vision of nothingness does not interest Pointer, who is very anxious to see the jointure of her wooden leg because, he says, it is what makes her different. She is horrified by his demand to see it because she takes care of it "as someone else would his soul, in private and almost with her own eyes turned away" (G, 192). Removing her leg, he removes the prop of her identity as he has removed her eyeglasses, her power of perception.

Hulga realizes that the leg is what makes her different, what distinguishes her from others, what has formed her whole being. When she gives him her leg, she gives him herself, her most essential being. Her hatred for her body and sexual fear become overpowering and she grows terrified of him as a man. "His eyes like two steel spikes, would glance behind him where the leg stood" (G, 193). His eyes penetrate her deepest self as she becomes his Vulcan-Venus, a deformed goddess to whom he offers a flask of whiskey, a pack of obscene playing cards, and a box of contraceptives. In effect he offers her a fundamentalist's vision of evil: gambling, whiskey, and sex. Hulga is shocked. She had thought of seducing him as a metaphor for corrupting his mind, turning him from his belief in Christ, that particular deformity that attracted her to him.

When Pointer takes her leg he tells her that he once got a woman's glass eye in the same way. The numerous references to eyes, glasses, and perception culminate in Pointer's assertion that he has seen through to nothing and believed in nothing since he was born. He has taken away her eyeglasses as well as her leg, the glasses that she peered through at a world inferior to that bubble of abstractions she called her own life. It was through her reading that she saw through to nothing, through averting her eyes from her own body and the natural world that she felt she pierced all illusions. She cannot confront the artifacts of negation: whiskey, condoms, and pornography. That glass eye Pointer stole from another woman who needed love may represent accurate perception, scientific reportage of what is. Reflecting the physical world, the glass eye sees all we can know.

The story ends as it began, with a view of the inexorable Mrs. Freeman, snouting among onions like a more stable Nebuchadnezzar. With her indomitable rigidity, her unqualified suspicion of everyone, and her love for grotesque physicality, Mrs. Freeman may be the only free woman of the story. Like Pointer she seems to have believed in nothing since she was born. Like him she is a collector of experiences, collating the number of times Glynese vomits, conjecturing the site of her pregnancy, praising the neck-popping of Carramae's chiropractor boy friend, and marveling at a woman who could conceive and give birth in an iron lung. This last, unnamed lady is perhaps the great heroine of all O'Connor's work, its only progeny who transcends the limits of her body.

Like "Good Country People," "A Temple of the Holy Ghost" develops the relation of spiritual to physical life. Its unnamed heroine may be a portrait of Joy-Hulga at twelve. Although it is more explicitly Catholic than any of the other stories in the canon, it embodies all of O'Connor's major themes and techniques. While it is less spectacular than "A Good Man Is Hard to Find," *Wise Blood,* or "The Life You Save May Be Your Own," its action is qualitatively of the same kind, showing, in a quieter way the same direction and impulses.

The plot of the story is simple. Two fourteen-year-old girls, Susan and Joanne, leave Mt. St. Scholastica, a convent school run by the Sisters of Mercy, to visit their aunt and twelve-year-old cousin for the weekend. The unnamed cousin considers them boy-crazy morons but seems resentful that they prefer each other's company to hers. At lunch the girls giggle and call each other Temple One and Temple Two, explaining that they have been told by Sister Perpetua, oldest nun at the convent, to remind ungentlemanly boys that they are temples of the Holy Ghost.

The conversation shifts to wondering who would be suitable escorts for the girls on Saturday night. The cousin first suggests Cheat, an old farmer who courts Miss Kirby, a spinster schoolteacher who lives with the aunt. She then suggests Alonzo Myers, a fat, smelly eighteen-year-old who drove them from Mayville. The girls become indignant. Later she suggests Wendell and Cory Wilkins, two Protestant boys of sixteen. Thinking the Wilkinses, who are going to be Church of God ministers, are safe escorts, the aunt invites them to come to dinner and take her nieces to a local fair. Arriving that evening with a guitar, they strum and sing Protestant hymns to the girls. Responding in turn, Susan and Joanne sing the *Tantum ergo*, which Wendell thinks "must be Jew singing." The cousin considers both boys as moronic as the convent girls and, calling Wendell a "big dumb Church of God ox," she refuses to eat with the couples and has supper with the cook instead. When they leave, she goes to her room and falls asleep.

Hearing the girls return at midnight, she wakes and tricks them into telling her what they saw at the fair by promising to describe how a rabbit gives birth. They say they saw a freak who was both man and woman and who said God created him that way. Although the child does not understand how someone can be both man and woman without having two heads, she is affected by God's having made the freak. Before she falls asleep again, images from the girls' description and the day's conversation flit through her mind. In the morning the girls are driven back to the convent, where everyone goes to Sunday mass. While returning home, Alonzo tells the child and her mother that the fair has been closed by the police at the request of some local preachers.[3]

The population of the story is a typical census taken in O'Connor's world: a mother either widowed or deserted, her difficult daughter, a lonely spinster schoolteacher, two pubescent Protestant boys, a fat eighteen-year-old boy, a stingy farmer, and a nun. Reappearing over and over in the stories, the strong mother and feeble, dependent daughter form what might be called a difficult daughter motif. In "A Circle in the Fire" Mrs. Copes's daughter is "a pale fat girl of twelve with a frowning squint and a large mouth full of silver bands." The child in "A Temple of the Holy Ghost" resembles her: "she doubled over laughing and hit the table with her fist and looked at the two bewildered girls while water started in her eyes and rolled down her fat cheeks and the braces she had in her mouth glared like tin." Somewhat older in "A Late Encounter with the Enemy," she appears as Sally Poker Sash, graduating from college at sixty-two. In "Good Country People," she is Joy-Hulga, "a poor stout girl in her thirties." In "Revelation" (*Everything That Rises Must Converge*) she is Mary Grace, disfigured by acne, "a fat girl of eighteen scowling into a thick book," and a student at Wellesley. All of these daughters pride themselves on being shrewder and smarter than their more gentle mothers. All are manipulative, aggressive, and brutal. Female counterparts of Motes, the Misfit, young Tarwater, and Johnson, their violence is more verbal than physical, perhaps because they are women. Using their minds as weapons, they inflict psychological rather than physical pain. In "A Temple of the Holy Ghost" they fight in microcosm and, in a world of children, wage the war of the present with the past, the physical with the spiritual. Almost wholly verbal and symbolic, the action of the story is the literalization of important statements. As spiritual "clichés come true with a vengeance," words become actions and objects.

Juxtaposed in characters and images, the forces of the present and past are neatly aligned. Joanne, Susan, and the Wilkinses champion optimism and hope, while their cousin and the hermaphrodite who takes form in her mind represent a grimmer past. Seen as a weapon of the present, the convent houses its optimism and hope while the freak's tent at the fair, a church of martyrs and temple of the Holy Ghost, praises deformity and resignation. It is a temple of the past that, moving through the backwoods to small country fairs, follows the route of O'Connor's saintly heroes.

An opposition between convent and tent also appears in color imagery. Images of whiteness cluster about the con-

vent. Since white is worn only on feasts of the Blessed
Virgin and the joyous feasts of Jesus, feasts which have
nothing to do with his suffering or martyrdom, the convent seems clearly a world without pain. On the other
hand, the hermaphrodite and child, the saints of the story,
are associated with red, color of the feasts of Christ's suffering and martyrdom. In effect, O'Connor paints the
present white, color of joy; and the past red, a color she
associates with martyrdom, ugliness and emotional intensity.

Estranged from the past, the present sees Christ as the
Wilkinses do—a lily of the valley, a spring flower associated with Easter and resurrection. The child sees him
crushed under his cross and his symbolic body, the Eucharistic sun, drenched in blood. Aquinas bears the standard of
the present, so often is he connected with the convent.
Looking so like Nietzsche's portrait of the priest, so perverse and so weak, the child-saint represents the grim physicality of the past. Like *The Violent Bear It Away* and
Wise Blood, this story hovers between the world of optimism, love, and hope, a world incomprehensible to the
child, and the overwhelming physical reality embodied in
the hermaphrodite.

Like her more active male counterparts, the child is an
unconventional heroine, a "saint" motivated by hate, an-
gered by happiness, and determined to be as verbally ugly
as she can. Like the Misfit, she attempts to prove her certainty—not of Christ but of herself—by harming others
and, using "sass" instead of bullets, aims at her cousins'
weakest points. Like the Misfit, she tries to end her confusion by aiming at the heart—by thwarting her cousins' need
for love and making them subject to her will. Unlike the
Misfit, she strikes out of a desire for power, not out of a
sense of justice.

As Motes might be called a parody of existential man, the child may be a parody of the priestly mentality drawn by Nietzsche in *A Genealogy of Morals*. She acts out of *ressentiment*, that hatred the weak feel for the strong, affirms the irrational over the rational, and, too weak to exert direct physical force, manipulates others obliquely. She has a propensity for the irrational which appears as an implicit assertion that her physical and moral ugliness is really a sign of her superiority. Considering the girls' prettiness and need for love as signs of stupidity, she sees her own homeliness as the badge of her brilliance. Envious and malicious, she is amused by the thought of Cheat or Alonzo Myers "beauing them around." She seems to laugh as much from pleasure in their certain disappointment as from a sense of the incongruity of the combination. Her sense of incongruity is highly selective. She cannot understand or accept her cousins' need for love and so enjoys thwarting it. Yet she can accept an even more irrational need to believe the body is a temple of the Holy Ghost although she is told this in a context where it is really funny, incongruous, and absurd. While she is confused by her cousins' interest in their bodies and clothes, she can accept on faith a freak's holiness, the sanctity of the hermaphrodite. A true O'Connor heroine, she thinks only the deformed, ugly, and pained are real.

Reason and faith oppose the present and past and appear in the story in two ways. Stated explicitly in the second stanza of the *Tantum ergo*, the relation of reason to faith is also embodied in imagery in numerous references to heads. In the hymn, reason is too weak to comprehend religious truth and only faith or intuitive knowledge can encompass it. Similarly, in imagery the head is part of worldly, physical reality to the extent that it is what defines sex for the child. She cannot imagine how anyone could be both man and woman without having two heads and tells her cousins that a rabbit gives birth by spitting its young out of its mouth. The organ of life in the world, the head, is associated with reproduction, with the body. The mind has no transcendent reality. In her fantasy, she cannot be destroyed by fire and only dies when the Romans cut off her head, her way of relating to the world. Intellect is associated with life in society—it governs one's relationships with people and can be used to manipulate them. Like Rayber's hearing aid, which cannot hear the apocalypse, it is a tool for social interaction, useless for understanding the absolute. If one goes to heaven at all, one goes, like the child in her fantasy, decapitated.

The humanistic world is represented in the story by Susan, Joanne, the Wilkins boys, and the convent. As Nietzsche came to mind in describing the saint of the story, so Aquinas may be associated with its humanists. Their home on Mt. St. Scholastica does suggest the most eminent scholastic of all. Wendell Wilkins, having sung a song about Jesus as a lily and friend, is called a "big dumb Church of God ox" by the girl because he does not understand the *Tantum ergo,* a hymn written by Aquinas. Significantly, St. Thomas was called the dumb ox as a nickname because he was fat and slow. As Protestants, the Wilkinses are associated with secular rather than papal power and may represent a modern attempt to reconcile religion with a melioristic society much as Aquinas tried to reconcile classical, humanistic values to those of his own time. Although they are mentioned as having sung "The Old Rugged Cross," what they sing in the story is a song about a melioristic Jesus, a kind of supernatural buddy. Using the hymn as a love song, they seem to court Susan and Joanne with it, casting "loving looks" at them while they strum and sing. Their religion seems very much a part of their social life and easily comprehended by a quotidian sort of thinking. Removed from any sense of the irrational source of God, they do not understand the *Tantum ergo*, which explicitly exhorts *praestet fides supplementum/ sensuum defectui*—let faith repair the defects of reason. In fact, they think it is "Jew talk," not Christian at all.

Susan and Joanne live in the convent. Described as a place where boy-crazy girls are sent to protect them from their own impulses, it seems a kind of social defense against incipient sexuality. Sister Perpetua's advice seems to use religion socially, to convert sanctity into an etiquette of preservation:

> Sister Perpetua, the oldest nun at the Sisters of Mercy in Mayville, had given them a lecture on what to do if a young man should—here they laughed so hard they were not able to go on without going back to the beginning—on what to do if a young man should—they put their heads in their laps—on what to do if—they finally managed to shout it out—if he should behave in an ungentlemanly manner with them in the back of an automobile. Sister Perpetua said they were to say, "Stop sir! I am a Temple of the Holy Ghost!" and that would put an end to it. [G, 18]

Epitomizing the goals of a melioristic society, the convent uses religion as a shield against the "stronger" passions, substituting an image of divine "parental" love for human sexual love. It uses reciprocal divine love—the Holy Spirit that is an emanation from both the Father and the Son—as a defense against unwanted human love. It "puts an end to it" and saves one from a real involvement, the kind of human interaction that is always painful in O'Connor's world.

The convent is a kind of humanistic perversion where belief in the perfectibility of man and happiness appear in an almost infantile form. It does not overcome or confront pain but simply denies it exists. Sister Perpetua's advice assumes the girls have no need for love and can be frozen in a perpetual childhood where they live in the womb of the Holy Spirit without human involvement. The convent is the agent of a world that wants to deny lust and brutality and reduce them to questions of propriety and gentility, much as Rayber and Sheppard want to ascribe their charges' defects to mistaken values and an unfortunate upbringing. As they use psychology to reduce the scale of the boys' evil to psychosocial maladjustment, so the convent uses religion to curb the more extravagant human impulses. It becomes a method and not a system of values.

Susan and Joanne remain substantially more interested in their legs than in the Holy Ghost. Evaluating Sister Perpetua's advice as a way of solving their problems, they find it absurd. They are trying to break out of the infantile painlessness of the convent—not to become martyrs but to become women. Obsessed with their individuality, their development as women, they joke about their anonymity before God as temples of the Holy Spirit. Calling each other Temple One and Temple Two, they laugh. The child is impressed by this anonymity and marvels that even Miss Kirby, that poor Miss Kirby who, like the girls, is guilty of the same stupidity of needing love, is a temple too.

Like the Misfit, Motes, Johnson, and young Tarwater, the child scorns the need for love and sees it in others with contempt. She ridicules the girls with their needs, their developing sexuality and awareness of their bodies. Having arranged their weekend by choosing their escorts, she lies to them about what the Wilkins boys look like in the hope they will be disappointed. She then has a daydream in which she saves the Wilkinses from Japanese suicide divers. They want to marry her, but instead of accepting them, she has them court-martialed. The fantasy suggests her envy of the girls and her need to be admired more than they. She wants to become what she pretends to despise. That she needs them to love her and then wants to punish them suggests a desire to be beyond the need for love, to assume a position of mastery in relation to the rest of the world and transcend its human impulses. In this, she is a potential Misfit or Motes, negating and avoiding love, murdering the grandmother when she feels a moment of compassion for him, abandoning Sabbath and the landlady.

The child is, in effect, able to prove she has no need for love by ridiculing it in others. Her inhumanity is proof of her superiority; and her hostility a way of gaining power. All her fantasies center on her domination of someone else —she is a fighter pilot who can court-martial at will, a doctor in an adult world associated with disease, and a martyr who can overcome lions. In reality she so wishes to have power over someone that she momentarily allies herself with her cousins. When, with their convent-trained voices, they sing the *Tantum ergo* and baffle the boys, she exults in the Wilkinses' bewilderment and insults them. Grateful not to be a victim, she later thanks God for not making her a dumb Church of God ox. Her sanctity is bound up with her sense of power, her ascendancy over others and her aggrandizement of herself. It has more to do with her need to assert herself than to gain some spiritual transcendence.

She feels someone has "given her a present" when she hears she is a Temple of the Holy Ghost; she does not feel more filled with God. Her saintliness begins to emerge after the *Tantum ergo* is sung. The hymn begins a series of religious references and symbols that occur throughout the rest of the story. In the stereotyped language of formal praise and prayer, the hymn suggests the child's mystic insight of the hermaphrodite's sanctity and the holiness of the Eucharistic sun. The hymn introduces "spiritual clichés" that are literalized as the story unfolds. Since the story seems to grow out of the hymn, it is useful to look at each stanza in turn before going any further. It begins:

> *Tantum ergo sacramentum,*
> *Veneremur Cernui:*
> *Et antiquum documentum*
> *Novo cedat ritui.*

Let us, bowing low, adore so great a sacrament and let the old ceremony give way to a new ritual, says the hymn. Dreaming of the freak's mass, the child creates a new ritual. Replacing the old ceremony of the convent, the mass in the tent substitutes a monster for the monstrance and revives a still older ritual. Taking the form of the dialogue or community mass, used in the first ten centuries of the church and revived in Europe by Pius XI, the freak's mass resurrects the past, making it powerfully, mystically survive in the present. A gothic veneration of ugliness and deformity as signs of grace, and of the fortunate nature of the fall, flourishes in the tent like a fossil suddenly brought to life. Yet it is a fossil damaged by the centuries and revived in its defective form. Although it can affirm the God who made it and permitted it to become damaged, it has lost a sense of heaven. It may praise God and prove its worthiness for heaven but heaven seems to have disappeared over the years.

> *Praestet fides supplementum*
> *Sensuum defectui*
> *Genitori, Genitoque*
> *Laus et jubilatio.*

Let faith repair the defects of reason! Praise and joy to the father and to the son, writes Aquinas. Obeying the exhortation, the child's faith makes her revere what she cannot understand—how something can be both man and woman.

> *Salus, honor, virtus quoque*
> *Sit et benedictio;*
> *Procedenti ab utroque*
> *Compar sit laudatio.* [G, 19]

Let there be might, honor, virtue, and blessings for the Father and for the Son! Let there be equal praise for the one who comes from both (i.e., the Holy Ghost), concludes the hymn.[4] The Holy Ghost, the reciprocal love of God and Christ, is ironically literalized in the body of the hermaphrodite. A *reductio ad absurdum* of multiplicity reduced to unity, the hermaphrodite embodies sexual union and reciprocal love. The exhortation to praise and venerate both Father and Son is fulfilled symbolically when, in the convent church, the congregation adores the raised monstrance. Safe and white in its golden receptacle, the Eucharist seems to suggest God the Father and the divine attributes of Christ. The symbol that ends the story, the sun drenched in blood, seems to be a parallel symbol of Christ as martyr and man.

The child, after the hymn is sung, unites with her cousins only to share their superiority to the Wilkinses. Refusing to dine with them, she will have no part of a communion feast and calls all four "stupid idiots." When they leave for the fair she goes to her room and, remaining in dimness, watches it grow smaller as the darkness thickens. As she stands alone in her room, images of enlightenment from the fair begin:

> At regular intervals a light crossed the open window and threw shadows on the wall. She stopped and stood looking out over the dark slopes, past where the pond glinted sil-

ver, past the wall of woods to the speckled sky where a long finger of light was revolving up and around and away, searching the air as if it were hunting for the lost sun. It was the beacon light from the fair. [G, 93]

Streaming from the fair past the woods, the finger of light may find the lost sun in the parallel symbol that ends the story—the Eucharistic sun that leaves a trail of blood over the same woods. A source of literal light, the beacon cuts the darkness of the child's room and introduces the image of the sun, which accumulates meaning as the story unfolds. Calliope music coming from the fair like an informal *Tantum ergo* recalls the past. Last year's fair had a tent for adults only covered with pictures of martyrs and enclosing something about medicine. As I have said, the tent is a metaphor for the adult future, a life of pain, sickness, and some hope of cure through medicine. Before the revelation of the hermaphrodite, the child thinks cure is possible, that there are doctors for the disease of life. She even prays "mechanically" in the convent church, "hep [*sic*] me not to be so mean" (G, 100), before her thoughts about the freak make her feel in the presence of God. After both revelations she seems less hopeful. The hermaphrodite's tent replaces the medicinal one as a metaphor for life and she seems aware not of the sanctity of men but of their physical qualities as she notices Alonzo's ears are "pointed almost like a pig's" (G, 100).

The memory of the tent bearing pictures of people "in tights, stiff stretched composed faces like the faces of the martyrs waiting to have their tongues cut out by the Roman soldier," is grimly literalized in the freak's tent, which contains a being martyred by God with his deformity, and by society with the loss of his church. Before its literalization, the memory initiates a fantasy about martyrdom. Because of her general malice and pride, the child knows she cannot be a Catholic saint, a self enlarged by God and able to love. She does think she can be a martyr, someone who, like Motes or the Misfit or old Tarwater, holds fast against a hostile world.

Showing her need for both Godhood and human love, the fantasy suggests the conqueror-victim theme. Illustrated above by young Tarwater's enthrallment of Bishop, this seems the only possible relation of the saint to others. His violence may not only be a way of responding to the present but, bringing him from the wilderness into the company of other men, may also be a way of reducing his loneliness. By inflicting pain on someone, he is able to establish some relation to him, and in a momentary act of murder or corruption, to feel some human contact. Inflicting no pain in her fantasy, the child is able to conquer and subdue without physical force by the violent significance of her presence, the power of her being. Thrown to the lions in a Roman arena, she subdues them without doing anything at all. Not only conquering them physically, she overpowers them spiritually and makes them love her. They like her so much she even sleeps with them.

Her daydream encounter with the lions may, in an ideal form, symbolize her relation to her cousins. Like the lions, Susan and Joanne are strong and beautiful in comparison with her. Although she can subdue and control them without physical force by insults and manipulation—by choosing their escorts and tricking them into revealing what they saw—she cannot make them like her. She has resented their paying her so little attention. In her daydream, the lions want to sleep with her but since, in reality, the lions are less friendly, she wants to hurt them by putting something nasty in their bed—perhaps herself.

Both versions of the dream suggest an overwhelming

need for power and love. In the first, she has the power of God to subdue and, simply by His presence, dominate the soul. While she cannot create love in the second version, she can subdue action to her will and think of ways to inflict pain. By putting something frightening and ugly in bed with them, she could establish some bond with them by leaving them a symbol of herself. By inflicting pain, she can assume power over them.

Unable to kill her with the lions, the Romans try to destroy her by fire, only to find she will not burn. Having overcome the lions and the flames, she dies only when, beheaded, she loses her means of gaining power in the world. Although she goes to paradise immediately after losing her head, her daydreams never go beyond this moment but keep returning to her encounter with the lions, the earthly situation that engrosses her. Wanting godlike power, she cares very little for heaven.

Beginning another train of religious images, the calliope music from the fair reminds her she has not said her prayers. Rarely feeling the presence of God while praying, she sees Christ at random moments when, imagining Him in His martyrdom, she sees a spectacle of suffering "on the long journey to Calvary, crushed three times under the rough cross" (G, 95). She becomes Christ "crucified" on Mt. St. Scholastica when, "as they were leaving the convent door, the big nun swooped down on her mischievously and nearly smothered her in the black habit, mashing the side of her face into the crucifix hitched onto her belt" (G, 100).

While the music and beacon from the distant fair have evoked religious images for the child, her cousins have been at the source of light in the freak's tent. They return giggling and unconverted, unconvinced of the hermaphrodite's sanctity. Projecting their own concerns, they describe the tent as a place of sexual isolation where men and women are separated by a black curtain and the freak moves from one side to the other, an ironic figure of sexual union. Fascinated and repelled by him, the girls cannot decide whether they like him or not. As the Misfit repays "love" with death, so the freak dampens their own sexual interest. In his "country voice, slow and nasal and neither high nor low, just flat" (G, 97), he threatens punishment for anyone who does not revere him:

> God made me thisaway and if you laugh He may strike you the same way. This is the way He wanted me to be and I ain't disputing His way. I'm showing you because I got to make the best of it. I expect you to act like ladies and gentlemen. I never done it to myself nor had a thing to do with it but I'm making the best of it. [G, 97]

No one laughs. Both accepting the will of God and assuming a certain control over it by threatening in His name, the freak silences everyone. No one knows whom God may punish, for His acts are unpredictable and, like the Misfit, he may strike anywhere. In telling about the freak, a revelation of God in sexual terms, the girls pose a riddle. Solving it by her faith, which does repair the defects of her reason, the child is affected by God's having made him. She cannot understand what the freak reveals when he lifts his dress but she is sure it is a revelation of God.

In the child's imagination, the hermaphrodite's tent blends with the one decorated with those stiff, painted figures that were so like Christian martyrs. They seem to come alive and fill the tent where "the men [were] more solemn than they were in church, and the women stern and polite, with painted-looking eyes, standing as if they were waiting for the first note of the piano to begin the hymn" (G, 98). Growing in her mind like a blossom of her own identity, the freak seems her saintly double just as Solace Layfield was Mote's social double. His unvisualized deformity is a metaphor for her own homeliness and worse moral blemishes that make the cook ask, "How come you be so ugly sometime?" As she associates her meanness with her mental superiority, so the freak she imagines wears his deformity as the mark of his sanctity. One has the impression he is holy simply *because* he is deformed. A celebration of deformity as well as sanctity, his mass emerges in her mind woven from her cousins' account:

> "God done this to me and I praise Him."
> "Amen. Amen."
> "But he could strike you thisaway."
> "But He has not."
> "Amen." "Amen."
> "Raise yourself up. A temple of the Holy Ghost. You! You are God's temple, don't you know? Don't you know? God's spirit has a dwelling in you, don't you know?"
> "Amen. Amen."
> "If any body desecrates the temple of God, God will bring him to ruin and if you laugh, He may strike you thisaway. A temple of God is a holy thing. Amen. Amen."
> "I am a temple of the Holy Ghost."
> "Amen."
> The people began to slap their hands without making a loud noise and with a regular beat between the Amens. . . .
> [G, 98]

Transformed into a priest leading a parody of the dialogue or community mass, the freak confers holiness on those who kneel before him. Eliminating the barrier between men and women, his church seems to offer complete communion in the reciprocity of the mass as they clap together rhythmically. In the convent scene that follows, the hermaphrodite's claim that he is a temple of the Holy Ghost is literalized in an image when, looking at the monstrance raised at benediction, the child thinks of him. After remembering the freak, she feels she is in the presence of God. In effect, her perception of the Holy Spirit, the freak, and the symbol of Christ are simultaneous. Because of this simultaneity there seems to be a moment of union between humanistic and religious values, the convent and the tent. As they leave the church, the nun swoops upon the child, mashing her face against the crucifix swinging from her belt. The encounter may parody the confirmation of faith ritual in which the bishop slaps the communicant to remind him that he must be willing to suffer anything for Christ. As a renewal of faith, it may also be another literalization of the new ritual mentioned in the first sentence of the *Tantum ergo*. Yet there is no effective communion in the convent, no reconciliation of the humanistic and religious.

While dressing to return to the convent, the girls exclaim, "Oh glory, Oh Pete! Back to the salt mines." They return to glory and St. Peter in secular terms. Their exclamation of "glory" and "salt" introduces the references to light and whiteness that increase as they drive toward the convent. "The sun was ivory and so white that the child could only see it through a screen of hair"; the child rejects a "moon-faced" nun while preserving a "frigid" frown; the Host is shining "ivory-colored" in its monstrance. The beacon light from the fair may have been searching for the lost sun, but the sun *en route* to the convent, so pure and so white, does not seem the one a hermaphrodite's finger of light would point to. It is too bright for human eyes—even those of a potential saint who must, screening it with her hair, see it through the medium of her self. So like the Eucharist in description, the sun seems to suggest pure divinity, God the Father and His Son before becoming man and mediating his godhead with humanity. The Eucharist in its golden monstrance, like the sun in the sky, is something unattainable. With their gleaming whiteness, they are connected with beauty, purity, and feasts of joy, with divine love and not human suffering. Since all but suffering are unknown to her, the child remembers the hermaphrodite when she looks at the Eucharist and shields her eyes when she sees the sun. If her faith is confirmed by the nun's embrace, it is because of the pain inflicted by the crucifix, by the martyrdom of Christ and herself. Ultimately, the convent remains a place of purity where the Eucharist is safely in its monstrance and the decorum of young girls is encouraged.

While returning from Mayville, the child learns the freak has been martyred a second time. In reporting that the police and local preachers have closed the fair, Alonzo places him among old Tarwater, Johnson, Motes, and the Misfit, that band of heroes so persecuted by the Authorities and exiled from society. With their modern, melioristic view of life, the preachers would rather refuse the freak a place among them than accept him as an embodiment of God's will. Like a corpse at a wedding, the tent is the "true" church in the modern world, indecently and immorally reminding man of ugliness and pain.

Producing another revelation of God, his second martyrdom has the same effect as his first. As she felt in the presence of God when, looking at the Host, she thought of the freak affirming his deformity, so she sees the Eucharistic sun after she has heard of his second trial and, looking at another example of deformity, noticed that Alonzo has "three folds of fat in the back of his neck and noted that his ears were pointed almost like a pig's" (G, 27). Like Mrs. Turpin, who, looking among her pigs for the truth about herself, has a revelation of heaven in her pigsty, she sees God only after a vision of ugliness.

When He does appear, God is colored red like the red of blood or the clay roads of the backwoods. Red has been associated with ugliness throughout the story. Susan and Joanne become ugly as they grow red with laughter, the Wilkins's faces become dark red with anger when the girls sing the *Tantum ergo*, and Cheat, the stingy farmer whose car smells like the last circle in hell, has a little fringe of rust-colored hair about his bald head. In imagery, Cheat is associated with the Host-sun at the end of the story. "His face was nearly the same color as the unpaved roads and washed like them with ruts and gulleys" (G, 86). When the sun sinks out of sight, it leaves a "line in the sky like a red clay road." As a trail left by God's blood, the road may not only be a mark of God but God himself. Associated with God and Hell, whose last circle, according to Dante, houses traitors, the convergence of imagery may suggest that God is an O'Connor saint on a grander scale. God, like life in Fitzgerald's memorable phrase, may be a cheat. As His saints are murderers and thieves, so God may be a traitor, one who didn't do what He said He did.

Red imagery culminates in the closing symbol as the child looks thoughtfully

> out over a stretch of pasture land that rose and fell with a gathering greenness until it touched the dark woods. The sun was a huge red ball like an elevated host drenched in blood and when it sank out of sight, it left a line in the sky like a red clay road hanging over the trees. [G, 101]

The red of blood and fire of the feast of martyrdom overpowers the white of the feasts of joy. The Eucharist is out of its monstrance but so drenched in blood that all its whiteness is colored red. As the brilliant ivory sun suggests pure divinity, so the bloodied sun suggests godhood tempered with manhood, Christ, the martyred God. The trail of blood it leaves like a road in the sky is the way to heaven paved by the blood of Christ. It lies not over the pasture land, over joy and repose, but over the forest, that wilderness of blood and martyrdom where O'Connor's saints are bred. The Misfit, Motes, Johnson, Tarwater, and his charge stumble along that road looking for the absolute. Those who get closest are, like the Misfit or Querry of Greene's *A Burnt-Out Case*, those in whom the disease of life has run its course and, having mutilated their humanity, left them able to act as freely as God. Although the child in "A Temple of the Holy Ghost" has just reached the beginning of the road and just seen where it lies, the freak she creates in her mind suggests her future self. She is the stuff O'Connor's saints are made of, an inchoate modern martyr.

Although O'Connor's heroes wander down a road paved with Christ's blood, they never reach a traditional Grail Castle. Despite their religious obsessions, they seem curiously without a transcendent sense of life. This is especially clear in "A Temple of the Holy Ghost," which paints a modern priest and O'Connor saint before a traditional Catholic backdrop. As the title implies, it should be a story about the dual nature of man formulated so well in Mrs. Turpin's question, "How can I be a pig and sacred too?" But in telling her tales, O'Connor reduces man's dual nature to a single element, flesh.

God may pitch his mansion in hermaphrodites, Misfits, and girls with braces, but it is difficult to accept that His presence in no way transforms them. But this is what much of the criticism of O'Connor's work would have us do. I think O'Connor describes man's piggish qualities while ignoring his spiritual ones. That Holy Spirit dwelling within the hermaphrodite does not allow him to transcend his deformity, it conforms to its shape much as Joy-Hulga's identity took the shape of her artificial leg. Making her see her soul in terms of her body, and not her body in terms of her soul, it welds her further to her flesh. Like her description of the convent, O'Connor's treatment of the Holy Spirit seems to be ironic, undercutting, as it does, its power as a traditional symbol of transcendence. All the outward signs of invisible grace shown by her characters are signs of mutilation, marks of deformity they cannot transcend. It may be that God can only be found in O'Connor's world in connection with finite, unredeemable human ugliness. Yet this seems unlikely to me.

What explodes from these stories is the sense that the Misfits, Shiftlets, Manley Pointers, and hermaphrodites are O'Connor's God. Their godliness resides precisely in their ability to escape from the chain of human involvements that binds Mrs. Crater to her daughter, Mrs. Hopewell to Hulga, and the child to her cousins. O'Connor's brutal heroes detach themselves from human problems by detaching themselves from life in human, familial terms. Over and over they reject human contact: Shiftlet evades his new family, Manley Pointer "destroys" the woman who wants to be his mistress, the hermaphrodite's deformity is so extreme that it frees him from the destructive forces of family life and places him beyond the pale of society at large. O'Connor's heroes are gods because they have won freedom from the nexus of human needs and longings that always, for O'Connor's characters, ends in overpowering frustration and rage. They are beyond sexual desire, love, or compassion. As the stories in *Everything That Rises Must Converge* will more explicitly show, the enduring crucifixion, the endless agony is close human contact. God, like the Misfit, is a force that can obliterate anguish, that can destroy all the "grandmothers" of the world—all the forces of tradition and family that bind people to each other.

4

The Enduring Conflict:

Parents & Children in

EVERYTHING THAT RISES
MUST CONVERGE

In her final collection of stories, *Everything That Rises Must Converge* (1965), O'Connor grew more concrete and more preoccupied with the physical cruelty of disease and with the more profound cruelty that exists between parents and children. For Flannery O'Connor, psychic savagery is embedded in the blood, not only metaphorically in the kinship of mother and child, but also in the living juice itself.

O'Connor took her title from Teilhard de Chardin, who believes that spirit, mind or soul are physical quantities, functions of the living organism that take part in the process of evolution. In effect, his conception negates any completely transcendent view of man. There can be no dualism of mind and body, according to Teilhard, but only a difference in the proportion of the physical, which he calls the "biosphere," to the spiritual, which he calls "nousphere." At point omega, the apex of human evolution, the nousphere and biosphere converge, blend, and enclose all life in an envelope of thought. In other words, at point omega, mind and body are fused and all human life is linked by an almost chemical bond existing between the atoms of spirit in each man. The universal envelope of thought Teilhard refers to is a kind of blanket woven from the atoms of spirit in each man, a living organism formed from particles springing from every human life.

O'Connor takes from Teilhard what she likes. She likes the idea that soul is a biological quantity, that it too is subject to physical processes. But for her the processes the body knows best are rarely processes of growth. Instead of evolving toward point omega, O'Connor's world stagnates or declines. In "Revelation" *Human Development* lands, rather appropriately, on the floor. Moreover, whatever atoms of spirit her heroes possess are unleashed in acts of violence; they never form anything so abstract as an envelope of thought. O'Connor takes one idea and ignores the intention and the mysticism of Teilhard. It is perhaps a distinctively O'Connor ploy to write some of her most powerful tales of human cruelty and destruction under the banner of a mystical Jesuit.

O'Connor never wrote about anything abstract. Her stories see evolution in specific and concrete terms as growing up. Growing up is not like the evolutionary spiralling toward nousphere Teilhard describes but, in genuine O'Connor style, it is a repetitive struggle with a strong parent. O'Connor makes Teilhard's abstractions concrete, shrinking the point of "convergence" from the universe to a microcosmic family, a family that usually consists of a widowed mother and her child. O'Connor's title, *Everything That Rises Must Converge*, becomes a banner for her tales of adolescent conflict: everyone who grows up must confront his parents.

In all but one of these stories, children grown well into adulthood are locked in a struggle with a parent they can neither love nor leave. In nearly all of them the struggle is resolved only by the "death" of the parent, often caused by the child. If the child is too crushed or weak to subdue his parent, he collapses. O'Connor is morally against parents and children killing each other—she even punishes children who rise up against their mothers. Yet what emerges most powerfully from her work is not the moral that it is wrong to want to destroy your parents. What explodes from these stories is the sheer agony of confronting a mother whose insensitivity renders you furious and whose politeness makes you impotent. However O'Connor resolves the conflict, it is clear that it is the conflict itself, far more than its resolution, that plagues her.

O'Connor's "heroes" are bound to their mothers by the immense physical dependency of weak, diseased or fearful children on their parents. She often presents her mothers from the point of view of a helpless child to whom they seem superhuman and omnipotent. They are, in fact, so powerful that O'Connor herself rarely lets her children destroy them directly. For example, Mary Grace so fears her mother's retaliation that she does not even let *herself* know she is angry with her. Many of these children feel so guilty about hating the mothers who have crippled them with "love" that they cannot even resent them directly. O'Connor's characters are often paralyzed by a mixture of hatred and guilt, by their yearning toward violent rebellion and their fear of losing their mother's protection or being punished in some other way. She deals with their mingled fear and guilt in a number of ways. In some stories she displaces their rage at their mothers onto other characters who are their mother's doubles. In other stories, she has her children's fantasies of revolt fulfilled by her children's more potent doubles. In still other stories, it is an impersonal force of nature that brings about the destruction her children are too weak or guilty to effect.

O'Connor's raging, passive children are championed by machines or animals, or by grotesque and Misfit Lochinvars who are so beyond the pale of human values and human ties that they can slay these dragon-mothers without fear or guilt. These odd instruments of their downfall O'Connor exalts with the quiet and replete joy of a woman who has been finally revenged. And like Mary Grace, whose fingers grip "like a baby's around her [mother's] thumb" after she knocks Mrs. Turpin to the floor, O'Connor's children can take their revenge and keep their mothers too. But it sometimes takes the combined force of Nature, Black Power, Technology and Social Progress to defeat these Southern ladies who can render you impotent with a smile or a kindly observation. Although they may seem as pathetic as they are pretentious, O'Connor clearly sees solid rock concealed beneath their fluffy, platitudinous surface.

None of O'Connor's children ever grows up to be a strong parent himself, but in two of her stories, "Everything That Rises Must Converge" and "A View of the Woods," O'Connor brings about a final equality between parent and child by rendering them both helpless. By the end of the title story, Mrs. Chestny's heart attack makes her as weak and dependent as her son, Julian. Yet O'Connor projects Julian's rage at his mother onto her Negro characters, who embody Julian's feelings about himself and his mother. The instrument of Mrs. Chestny's downfall is a rather militant black woman who refuses to let Mrs. Chestny's condescending smile humiliate her and will not let her son accept Mrs. Chestny's patronizing offer of a bright penny. In effect, Mrs. Chestny is overcome by a race she and her ilk have treated like exploited children for several generations. The black woman has reached a sudden, cataclysmic maturity that fulfills Julian's fantasies of revolt. She is the "heroine" of the story.

Grandfather and granddaughter struggle against each other in "A View of the Woods." As in "Everything

That Rises Must Converge," they achieve a kind of equality through becoming equally helpless—the one from age, the other from youth. Although they do succeed in killing off each other, they are both defeated by the giant machine that dominates the story: the steam shovel that has, for so many people from O'Connor to C. Vann Woodward, become the symbol of innovation and progress in the South. Some of O'Connor's mothers are so strong it takes the power of nature to defeat them. Mrs. May in "Greenleaf" is so much more potent than her sons that it takes a bull to subdue her. Even the bull is successful only because the sun has helped to lull her into lowering her guard.

O'Connor's less fortunate children find no champion in black progress, economic development, or nature. Asbury Fox in "The Enduring Chill" is too weak and crushed—by both fever and life—to retaliate against his mother, a woman who has worked very hard to blind herself to what he is and what he feels. He is never able to get through her impenetrable politeness and cheeriness. Even in his most potent fantasy, he feels he has to die to make her think about him as a person and not as an extension of herself. He even intends to leave her a letter—to read after his death—to help her see the truth. But he can never really talk back to her directly. He does not die of his fever as he would like, but instead is forced to live with it in the enduring chill of his mother's presence.

In "The Comforts of Home" Thomas shoots his mother, but only by accident. Acting on the advice of his dead father, whose voice encourages him to rid the house of the girl his mother has taken in, he raises the gun to shoot the girl and kills his mother instead. Thomas is too weak to leave his mother or to assert himself against her wishes without some outside force (the hallucinated voice of his dead father) encouraging him to confront her. Even then, he can only do it indirectly by confronting the girl who is, perhaps, her double.

"Revelation" is one of O'Connor's most brilliant stories. As in "The Comforts of Home," O'Connor handles rage at a mother indirectly as she has Mary Grace behave politely to her less inhibited mother, but permits her to grow more and more enraged by her mother's double, Mrs. Turpin. Like the black woman Mrs. Chestny would like to keep down, or the scrub bull Mrs. May would like to get rid of, or the steam shovel that engorges itself on Southern land, or the voice of a dead man who was potent in life, Mary Grace is the instrument of her "mother's" downfall. She is one of those Misfits, one of those despised victims, one of those worms who suddenly turns. And even though O'Connor has her collapse immediately after she hurls a book at Mrs. Turpin, she does not really punish her act so much as she vindicates it. As my discussion of the story will show, "Revelation" is a tale in praise of violence.

The violence that dominates nearly all of these stories is the slow violence of disease: the physical or psychic weakness that binds children to their mothers. The alternatives seen by Hazel Motes as he looked through the train window at nothingness, or back at the porter whose father died from a pig's cholera, scarcely exist in this collection. All of O'Connor's universe is a trap where everyone is engulfed in his own body. What rises and converges in many of these stories is blood itself, blood that goes through a very literal struggle of the heart.

What rises and converges in "Everything That Rises Must Converge" is Mrs. Chestny's blood pressure. Blood converges in a heart attack for this lady, who, like Joy-Hulga, Manley Pointer, and old man Fortune, has heart trouble.[1] Julian, her son, has the sort of heart trouble all O'Connor's characters have—he suffers from "ice in the blood," from a pervasive emotional death. At the opening of the story, he waits impatiently for his poor but pretentious mother to dress for her exercise class at the Y. He resents having to take her there but feels he is obliged to go because she so fears integrated buses and is so intent on losing weight because of her blood pressure. She consoles him on the way for being just an unsuccessful writer who sells typewriters with clichés like "Rome wasn't built in a day" and by reminding him that he is a Chestny. Neither fact makes him feel better.

On the bus, Mrs. Chestny begins complaining about integrated buses to a white woman sitting near her. To annoy her, Julian tries to start a conversation with a Negro man. A Negro woman and her little son get on, delighting Julian when he notices the woman wearing a hat identical to his mother's. Mrs. Chestny makes a number of affable, condescending remarks to her and her son and, after they leave the bus, offers the child a penny. Infuriated, the Negro woman strikes her. Gloating over his mother's misfortune, Julian pursues her as she stumbles along the street, telling her she deserves the blow. Mrs. Chestny suffers a heart attack and dies, not recognizing Julian as her son.

Like "The Life You Save May Be Your Own," "Good Country People," and "A Temple of the Holy Ghost," "Everything That Rises Must Converge" develops the relation of the mind to the body. Unreflecting strong plasm (biosphere) appears as Mrs. Chestny and the thought (nousphere) that is linked to it is Julian, an intellectual bound to his mother yet despising her pettiness and her prejudice. The story evolves as a gradual expansion of consciousness as Julian and his mother move from fantasy to reality.

Both Julian and his mother come most alive in their fantasies. Mrs. Chestny sees her own life through a kind of haze formed by her recollections of her family plantation, the Godhigh mansion, and the Chestny name, which define for her the old South. She sees her son, Julian, less as he is than as she thinks he ought to be as a Chestny and a Southern Gentleman. Julian's fantasies are connected almost entirely with his own origins and heritage. The Godhigh mansion is the Edenic plantation of the old South, where he is surrounded with beauty and cared for with grace. Like the antebellum house the old grandmother wants to find in "A Good Man is Hard to Find," it exists outside of time and place like a Grail castle that can be experienced only as a suffusion of peace. Julian's fantasies about himself as the mansion's heir emerge from his need for his mother. Through her he knows the mansion as he knew the world of his own childhood, communicated by a doting woman.

In a more real way, Julian is obsessed by his mother. He despises himself for needing her and feels nothing but guilt for his inability to leave her or respect her. The bond between them may appear in the story in the profusion of images of blood, blood colors, and bruises. Mrs. Chestny's blood pressure is high, her hat is purple and green velvet, the colors of a bruise. While she pins on her hat, Julian feels wounded and pinned to the door. Even the landscape is the color of congealed blood—the sky a "dying violet," houses are bulbous, liver-colored, and bounded by a collar of dirt. The world about Julian is a world of blood and earth, totally organic, engulfing even inanimate things in a kind of mortality.

Julian's relation to his mother and the past she represents is implied in his name. He is an apostate Julian raised to be a gentleman—someone with an inner worth that exists independently of possession of a mansion. Although raised as a Christian, and a Chestny, who should be able to forgo worldly pomp because of his great spiritual wealth, Julian still yearns after the old gods, or, more specifically, the old Godhighs.

When he is likened to St. Sebastian, pinned to the door by his mother's hatpin as the saint was pinned by arrows, his real situation is implied. His mother has raised him to fulfill her fantasies about her own life, and to be an ornament she can use at will. Having consistently ignored what he is and forced him into the shape of her own dream, she is an immensely controlling woman whose arrows have pinned down her son, even if she veiled them in an amiability distinctively Southern. While Julian-Sebastian is "saved" from entirely fulfilling her expectations, as St. Sebastian was once cured of his wounds, he lives to suffer a worse fate. As Sebastian was beaten and thrown into a sewer to die, so Julian's illusions—the "mental bubble" in which he preserves his image of himself apart from his mother's sentimentality and his own sense of failure—meet a bad end. Without them he is beaten, deprived of all his defenses, and left in the morass of his own human needs and his almost total dependency on his mother. As St. Sebastian was left in a sewer, so he is left in a repository of a kind of mortality.

Mrs. Chestny's chatter on the bus introduces a theme running throughout the collection: the disorder of the modern world. The desegregation of buses and the general rise of the Negro seem to her so much chaos, a chaos in which the old and the young, the present and the past, most violently collide. The "bottom rail is on the top," Mrs. Chestny says, as Mrs. Turpin in "Revelation" will repeat at greater length. In "Everything That Rises Must Converge," Mrs. Chestny's comment about the rise of the Negro applies to her son as well. Julian may be the "bottom rail"—the smallest, most childlike person in her world, who is striving to be on top, to be larger than his parent. In

the course of the story, he imagines himself in three roles in
which he could stand in this relation to her. He is first the
heir of the Godhigh mansion and the only one left to bear
the Chestny name. He is essential to his mother, who has no
way of implementing her wishes without him. Secondly,
he is the friend of a Negro doctor, in effect, is the Negro
doctor himself. Despised and enslaved by the Godhighs
and Chestnys, the Negro doctor in his fantasy is the only
one who can save the dying Mrs. Chestny. He then imagines himself as the husband of a Negress, a woman he has
chosen explicitly to replace his mother in his life and whom
he uses to express his contempt for her.

In his fantasies and in his attempt to start a conversation
with a black man on the bus, Julian allies himself with a
race in the process of confronting the authority that has
oppressed and humiliated them for so many years. He is
truly happy to see his mother become "purple-faced"
when he talks to a Negro and is still happier when the sight
of the black woman wearing an identical hat turns her eyes
a "bruised purple." If the black woman can rebel by own-
ing a Chestny hat, Mrs. Chestny can retaliate with a condescending smile. She looks amusedly at the woman "as if
the woman were a monkey that had stolen her hat." As
Mrs. Chestny has treated her son like an eternal infant, a
monkey she has trained to fulfill her needs and expectations, so she tries to infantilize the black woman with an
amused smile and an offer of a bright new penny to her
son. While Julian is sufficiently crushed and dependent on
his mother to be subdued by her smiles and low expectations of him, the black woman is made of sterner stuff. In
her mounting fury she hits Mrs. Chestny with her handbag.
"If you know who you are, you can go anywhere," said
Mrs. Chestny to her son before boarding the bus. The
trouble with Mrs. Chestny is that she refuses knowledge of

anyone else, especially her son and his black, female counterpart. That the black woman is in some way related to Mrs. Chestny is suggested by a number of resemblances: she not only wears a Chestny hat, she too suffers from a heart attack, an attack of explosive anger at her humiliation, an attack that says quite clearly that she is as proud and as dissatisfied at the state of things as Mrs. Chestny. Her blood, like Julian's and Mrs. Chestny's, has been "given one ounce of pressure too much." All three will suffer heart attacks in the story. All three are engulfed in a common horror: the agony of having to live with each other from day to day, the slow abrasive wrath that comes from a life of oppressing and being oppressed.

When the black woman strikes her, Mrs. Chestny loses all sense of the present. She forgets who she is—a Chestny who has been beaten by a black woman—and she remembers who she was. As her son accuses her of being childish, she slips back into her own childhood as a Godhigh and calls for her landowning grandfather and her Negro nurse. She no longer recognizes Julian as her son. Nor is she familiar to him. "He was looking into a face he had never seen before." In effect, she really becomes the child he has told himself she was and can no longer protect him, control him with her fantasies, or even provide him with something to hate. Her remaining eye "fixed on him, raked his face again, found nothing and closed."

Shouting for help, Julian's voice becomes thin as a child's. The black woman's blow not only shatters Mrs. Chestny's sense of who she is; it also destroys Julian's illusions about his own strength. The story ends when "the tide of darkness seemed to sweep him back to her, postponing from moment to moment his entry into the world of guilt and sorrow" (E, 23), which is perhaps the moment of birth. If Julian's birth as a man has been postponed by his mother's suffocating love, it is now postponed by the equally shattering absence of her protection.

The convergence at the end of the story is almost entirely literal. Mrs. Chestny becomes childlike; Julian hears his own childish voice echoing down the street. The tide of darkness that sweeps him toward her is the tie of blood, a kind of unsevered umbilicus. Both these children of the old South are relics who crumble in the face of the future the black woman suggests. Both are powerless before the black woman's violence. One dead, one barely born, both defenseless and engulfed in darkness, they confront each other with a kind of equality. —*Stop*

Like Mrs. Chestny, Mr. Fortune in "A View of the Woods" suffers from heart trouble and total insensitivity. He sincerely believes his nine-year-old granddaughter is an exact replica of himself, a double who shares his contempt for her father and who has no will of her own. He is attached to her without knowing her at all and is shocked to learn that she is not an extension of himself.

Past and present not only converge on each other as Mr. Fortune confronts Mary Fortune Pitts, they collide as a result of the economic development of the South, a revolution not of blacks but of business. The story opens near a synthetic "red corrugated" lake made by the electric company. Old Mr. Fortune and his granddaughter sit watching a steam shovel clear the land. While Mr. Fortune speaks in praise of progress, the child watches the machine to be sure it keeps within its boundaries.

When Fortune tells Mary he wants to sell the land in front of their house for a gas station, the girl is shocked. She objects because her father grazes his cows on the lawn, her six brothers and sisters play there, and the station will block their view of the woods across the road. Fortune cannot see why she should care about her father since her father beats her, behavior he believes the child should not permit. He tries to persuade her with promises of a boat and ice cream, but has no success. When he sells the land to Tilman, who will build on it, the girl begins to wreck Tilman's store.

Fortune feels he has no recourse but to whip her as her father does, to beat her into respecting her wishes. The heart of Fortune becomes enlarged with the pain of wronged love as he drives toward the spot in the woods where her father beats her. He strikes her once or twice without conviction. She turns on him, jumps upon him and begins kicking and biting him until she overwhelms him. When she tells him that she is not a Fortune but pure Pitts, he becomes so furious that he forces her under him, strangles her and hits her head on a rock. Afterward, he dies of a heart attack.

The theme of the story emerges through two powerful images: the steam shovel that begins and ends the tale and the clay on which it feeds. An image of progress, the machine is an insatiable monster whose "big disembodied gullet gorge[s] itself on clay, then, with a deep sustained nausea and a slow mechanical revulsion, turn[s] and spit[s] it up (E, 55). Clay, as the stuff of life, is one of the central images of the story. It is the flesh of the land, exposed when the trees that cover it are cleared away. Old Mr. Fortune liked to think of his granddaughter "as being thoroughly of his clay." And it is over the sale of clay—the earth in front of the farmhouse—that the dispute begins. The story ends with alternating images of life and death, clay and a blank sky full of nothing.

The child is Mr. Fortune's double made of his own clay. Their relationship has gone on forever. She is his granddaughter, named after his mother, who died in childbirth. A double reflection of his own image, she is at once the mother he never had and the daughter he has produced, an embodiment of his own self-love. Her father, Pitts, is the pit, the gulf between what he would like to believe and the reality he cannot escape. Everything Fortune hates is represented by Pitts, who has failed at everything, who is a reminder of the grave, that final pit of mortality, and whom Fortune always thwarts by keeping him poor and dependent on him. The old man's future disappointment is projected literally in the beatings Pitts gives Mary. Pitts beating Mary Fortune is O'Connor's tableau of Fortune succumbing to defeat. It reminds the old man that he cannot prevent the beatings and that the child he sees as an idealization of himself is as helpless from youth as he is from age.

On the other hand, Pitts beats the child *because* the child is Fortune's double and he can use her to hurt the old man who keeps him so financially weak that he cannot attack him directly. The three are bound together by blood, by money, by the tight bond of cruelty they inflict on each other in the woods. O'Connor's view of the woods is a view of the wilderness of human life, of the horror of youth (Mary), of middle life (Pitts), of age (Fortune), of the pain of needing either money or love or care from other people.

Mary Fortune Pitts is the victim of both men. She is used by her grandfather much as young Tarwater is used by the old prophet as a means of extending his will into the future. She is used by her father as the instrument of his own revenge. She is both a projection of Pitts's rage and of Fortune's hopes, as ambiguous and impersonal a character as the wilderness she loves.

The woods are the most ambiguous element in the story. Mr. Fortune cannot understand why they should be of such value to the child or why she should object to their being blotted out by the gas station. When he tries to understand, his consciousness is loosened and, freed from its preoccupation with progress, it feels in the presence of some mystery. "He saw it, in his hallucination, as if someone were wounded behind the woods and the trees were bathed in blood" (E, 71). The someone who is wounded may be Mary, who has been beaten by her father in those woods. To blot out the view may be to blot out the sight of her most significant experience, the one in which she in some way connects with her father and asserts that she is not an extension of Mr. Fortune, but Mary Fortune *Pitts*.

As Mary attacks her grandfather, she turns from an idealized self-image into a negative one. In effect, she shows Fortune what he is to the Pitts family—someone who takes advantage of feebleness and poverty. Coming at him from all sides, her face a mirror of his own, she bites and gnaws like a conscience stirred into life after a long sleep. His heart expands as he incorporates into it the aspects of himself that he has denied. Fortune tries to escape his growing heart, and to flee the woods, the wilderness of his own humiliation. His heart attack is an attack of consciousness as well as an attack of conscience. But knowledge, like introspection in O'Connor's world, always kills.

As his consciousness swells, he can see through the trees an opening onto the lake where the sky is reflected blankly in the water. His mind moves toward it away from the mortality of the woods. Yet he has no way to cross into that blankness, no way to swim away from his body. He is trapped in the pit of his old age, immobilized within his mortality, left with the image of the monster machine gorging itself on clay, consuming his own body like the passage of time.

In "The Enduring Chill," life for O'Connor is no more than a fever in matter. The steady rising of the blood of

"Everything That Rises Must Converge" appears as Asbury's undulant fever detected from a blood culture.[2] His fever rises and falls, reaching an apex in his recognition, in a stain on the ceiling, of the Holy Ghost, symbol of reciprocal love, poised above his head with an icicle in his beak. The icicle held above him like a sword is the chill of life, looming above him as his mother stands by his bed.

He comes home to die from his chilling fever with a letter which will reveal himself to his mother and shatter her illusions. Yet he learns the source of his own sickness only because of her intervention. The taint in his blood was literally caused by his mother's milk: Asbury was infected by milk from her farm. Trying to make allies of her Negroes, he encouraged them to drink her milk, although she forbade it, and drank it himself to encourage their rebellion. Engorged with his mother's unpasteurized milk, he became ill.

As Dr. Block says appreciatively of the cause of his mysterious fever, "Blood will tell." Part of what it tells is that the source of his disease is his attachment to his mother. Asbury, who is hoping to die so that he will have some effect on her, finds he has become ill from his attempt to rebel against his mother, an attempt in which he, like Julian, tries to ally himself with blacks. But his mother's Negroes are either not at all militant or are knowledgeable about unpasteurized milk. Mrs. Fox has not only shrewdly insulated herself from the world of integrated buses, and surrounded herself with Negroes out of the old South, she is in general made of sturdier stuff than Mrs. Chestny. She never becomes childlike or frightened. Instead of introducing her to reality, Asbury is drawn into her fantasy of omnipotence. When she asks, "Do you think for one minute . . . that I intend to sit here and let you die?" Asbury "felt the first distinct stroke of doubt" (E, 101).

Hoping to restore his equilibrium, and resenting his mother's cheeriness, Asbury demands to talk to a Jesuit. And his mother actually finds him one. But as Julian calling for help sees a man come out of a lighted building and walk the other way, so Asbury's potential savior turns out to be another ineffectual male, a stock personage in O'Connor's world. Perhaps both the man walking in the other direction and the priest who is half deaf, half blind, and totally inattentive are images of God.[3] But they are also images of the husband and father, those potent men who are as hard to find as Christ in O'Connor's world.

"Greenleaf" repeats the theme of "Everything That Rises Must Converge" and "The Enduring Chill" from the point of view of the mother. We meet Mrs. May, who, having forced herself into an eternal spring with curlers and face creams, lives in fear of the passage of time. She "keeps" her youth by making sure her sons never grow up enough to leave her milk farm.

Her son Wesley had had rheumatic fever and "Mrs. May thought that this was what had caused him to be an intellectual." Neither he nor his insurance-agent brother, Scofield, want to have anything to do with the farm. But neither of them leaves it. Like Julian and Asbury, Wesley dreams of leaving the farm and going to Paris and Rome but cannot even reach Atlanta because of his need for his mother, a dependency whose symbols are his weakened heart and salt-free diet. Since Mrs. May is also ridiculed by her hired hand, Mr. Greenleaf, whose sons are successful dairymen, she is surrounded by hostile males who accept her care and wages but, she feels, give nothing but abuse in return. She tries to protect herself from them by constant work. She is, in fact, so busy doing everything herself that she never sees how much her contempt for Scofield's work as a salesman of the kind of insurance "that only Negroes buy," and the ridicule she bestows on all of Wesley's aspirations, contribute to their hatred of the farm. She sweetly conveys how much a failure she considers Scofield by reminding him that no "nice girl wants to marry a nigger-insurance man" (E, 29).

Although Mrs. May taunts her sons with their failure, it is clear she could not endure it if they were strong or successful. She compares them—to their disadvantage—to the sons of her hired hand, Mr. Greenleaf, who not only are healthy, but who have also been to Paris and returned to become successful dairy farmers. While she envies them bitterly, the story shows she fears these potent men even more.

We first meet Mrs. May in her curlers while the Greenleaf bull is thrusting his horns beneath her bedroom window. The action of the story is her attempt to kill or drive away the bull.[4] When she goes to the Greenleaf's successful dairy farm, she enters an awesome, frightening, phallic universe where "the sun was directly on top of her head, like a silver bullet ready to drop into her brain" (E, 42). Earlier in the story as the bull thrusts against her bedroom, she dreams that the sun is a kind of thrusting bull—a large stone grinding a hole on the outside wall of her brain. As the sun tries to burn an opening in the treeline, it grows narrower and narrower and becomes like a bullet. "Then suddenly it burst through the treeline and raced down the hill toward her" (E, 47).

She wakes to the sound of the bull nibbling at the shrubs around her house. Similarly, as soon as she relaxes in the field, letting the sun drift into her, the bull charges toward her, burying his horns in her lap. What she sees last is like Hazel Motes's last vision, a world that is nothing but sky, nothing but blankness.

The scrub bull whose sperm will harm Mrs. May's cows,

like the man walking away from Julian and the useless priest, is one of O'Connor's ambiguous symbols. He may be Christ, a god wearing a prickly crown, as he gnaws at Mrs. May's shrubs, yet his crucifixion of the lady on his horns results in a perception of nothingness. In the context of the story, he seems an equally ambiguous image of time, an ironic comment on virility, and Mrs. May's idea of potent men as hostile and destructive. Like the Misfit, the bull is one of those bad men who are so easy to find in O'Connor's South, where men are either diseased, infantile, or murderers.

"The Comforts of Home" is O'Connor's most explicit description of the bond between a powerful mother and her effeminate, dependent son[5]—an Oedipal fantasy on the theme of "Everything That Rises Must Converge," "The Enduring Chill," and "Greenleaf." One of the discomforts of home is Thomas's mother's provocative love for her son. Head of a local historical society, Thomas at thirty lives with his mother, who provides him with good dinners, a place to write his histories, and an electric blanket. When his mother reads about a nineteen-year-old girl, Star Drake, who has been arrested for passing bad checks, she pityingly decides to take her a box of candy. She becomes interested in the girl, has her paroled in her care, and takes her into her own home when she is thrown out of her boarding house for drunkenness.

Thomas is enraged with his mother for disrupting his routine. Unable to teach her a lesson by leaving home, he tries to plant a gun in the girl's handbag, and report her possession of it to the sheriff in the hope that she will be sent back to jail. Instead, the girl returns the gun to his den and catches him when he tries to put it back in her bag. As he begins to insist that he has just found the gun in her bag, he hears his dead father's voice urge him to fire it at the girl. She lunges toward him and he fires but kills instead his own mother, who has intervened to protect the girl. The sheriff appears in time to see Thomas and Star standing over his mother's body. He assumes they are about to fall into each other's arms.

The story opens with images of Thomas's overwhelming passivity. Its opening words, "Thomas withdrew," define his actions throughout the story. He peers out from behind a curtain, does not know where any of the artifacts of mobility are—cannot find a suitcase or a portable typewriter and, like his electric blanket, can only survive when firmly plugged into his mother's house. When he feels he has no alternative but to leave, "he was like a man handed a knife and told to operate on himself if he wished to live" (E, 135). His feeling suggests an image for his tie to his mother—a tie like an umbilicus of food, warmth, and comfort he cannot cut.

Star Drake, whose real name is Sarah Ham, enters the house as aggressively the Greenleaf bull penetrates Mrs. May. Her laugh is like a bullet that "shoots up," moving like a "bolt of electricity." She intrudes into his room at night, determined to sleep with him. After driving her out with a chair, he complains to his mother, who merely accuses him of a defect in charity, asking him how he would feel if he were a "nimpermaniac" whom no one would take in. As she asks him to put himself in the girl's place, he begins feeling literally as though he is Star. He feels a "loathing for himself as if he were turning slowly into the girl."

Star-Sarah, ushered in so monumentally by Thomas's mother, may be her double. She has attracted her by tales of her fantastic sexual encounters, her seduction, her pursuit by perverts and sadists, and her insatiable sexual desire. Star's moral innocence is the opposite of Thomas's mother's equally fierce and relentless innocence, a form of moral blindness existing behind the banner of charity rather than psychology. Star-Sarah is, like so many of the doubles in O'Connor's fiction, a projection of two aspects of a single personality. As Star she is the shining sexual fantasy of Hollywood. As Sarah she suggests the matriarch of the Bible, wife of Abraham, who punishes the sexuality of her husband with Hagar by casting out his mistress and unborn son.

Star may be an expression of the mother's sexual self. That she brings her into her own house may express both her own sexual longing and her ambivalence. In one way, she uses Star both to provoke her son sexually and to taunt him with his own passivity, to point out a lack of masculinity she herself has fostered. Her demand that he see the world through the girl's eyes, feel it with feminine feelings, puts him through a kind of impotent agony in which he becomes more infantile and feminine while in some way longing to be more manly.

Thomas begins hearing the voice of his father, which may be the voice of the dead, potent male in himself. His father's voice reminds him that every house should have a loaded gun in it, yet suggests an oblique use of the loaded gun. Planting the loaded gun in Star's handbag, he tries to use her possession of it against her. In other words, he tries to use her "potency" to destroy her, much in the way his mother used his sexuality to destroy him. Making him so fearful of the longing she encouraged, she has caused him to crush his own manhood and remain in an extended infancy.

The conflict between him and Star emerges as a peculiar kind of sibling rivalry with a sexual bent. She is like a devil-child brought home by his mother, her comments like devil-children, "denizens with personalities, present though not visible, who might any moment be expected to shriek or rattle a pot (E, 119). Her laughter, expletive "fabulous!," bowleggedness, and her almost chronic spraddle-legged position make him think she is like a terrible child with the worst form of moral innocence—guiltlessness. So guilty himself about his own masculinity, he sees her lack of inhibition as the most evil thing about her.

His most sexual act, planting the gun in Star's bag, is described in images of blood, pain, and guilt. When he is caught, his hands hang helplessly at the wrists as if "he had just pulled them up out of a pool of blood" (E, 140). He is literally caught red-handed, in an image that both suggests the redness of blood, the blood-bond with his mother, and associates sexuality with wounding, inflicting pain. The shot he fires extends this image. He hears it as a sound that will end evil, "shatter the laughter of sluts until all the shrieks were stilled and nothing was left to disturb the peace of perfect order" (E, 141). In a sense, he may want to kill what is Star in his mother, who, though nameless, may well be Sarah-Star herself. By killing a mother who has helped destroy him sexually, yet taunts him with his effeminacy, he may hope to destroy what he finds threatening and fearful in her while preserving what comfort she gives him. When he fires that shot, he wants to kill the Star in her while preserving her Sarah qualities, to purge the matriarch of the slut.

When Farebrother enters and sees Star and Thomas standing over the dead woman, he assumes they are about to collapse into each other's arms. Despite the obvious implication, the ending may be ambiguous. They are about to collapse perhaps because both of them depended on the old woman for life. Star can no longer live now that "Sarah" is dead and Thomas, having lost his only support in the world, can only fall down.

"Revelation" develops the theme of conflict between parents and children in a wider, more complex way than any of the previous stories. The confrontation between a mother and daughter makes Mrs. Turpin confront herself. The complexity of the story comes less from its action than from its themes and imagery. It opens with the entrance of Mrs. Ruby Turpin and her husband, Claud, into a doctor's waiting room. While waiting for Claud's bruised leg to be examined, Mrs. Turpin talks to a stylish, respectable lady who is there with her daughter, an ugly Wellesley student named Mary Grace. The older women exchange small talk and banalities while Mary reads a book called *Human Development* and is irritated by the discussion. She begins staring at Mrs. Turpin, who has begun an effusion of thanks to Jesus for making her what she is. Hurling her book at Mrs. Turpin, she calls her an old wart hog, and tells her to go back to hell where she came from. Mrs. Turpin falls, bruised by the book but still more stunned by the girl's words. She remembers them at home and goes to her hog pen, looking for the nature of her resemblance to a wart hog. Finally, she has a vision of people marching to heaven through a sheet of fire.

"Who do you think you are?," the question Mrs. Turpin shouts over her hog pen to her fields, reverberates throughout the story, summing up all its themes. Mrs. Turpin's adventures provide an almost explicit statement of O'Connor's view of the self. She paints her picture in two ways: with images of animals and machines and with doubles who objectify different aspects of the same self. Mrs. Turpin's ideal self-image is the stylish, respectable mother of Mary Grace, her darker self is the respectable "nigger woman," her darkest self is the wart hog—the old sow Mary Grace says she is.

The doctor's waiting room in which the story opens

may be an image for the world, a microcosm of an O'Connor society where everyone is sick. It contains Mrs. Turpin and her husband, small farm owners, the Wellesley girl, who may have learned to be ugly up North, her affable mother, a dirty child, his white-trash mother, his grandmother in a gunny-sack dress, and an old man who seems to be dead. Everyone waits for the nurse with the high-stacked blonde hair to call them in for judgment. The outer world, seen through the curtains as a revolving shadow, penetrates the waiting room only when a Negro boy brings food for the nurse and as the radio plays pop and gospel music. The fruits of life seem available to the nurse but only its pieties exist for that spectrum of Southern society O'Connor presents.

The use of a doctor's waiting room as an image for society suggests that recurring seventeenth-century metaphor for the world as a hospital where one waits to be healed by Christ, the wounded surgeon. While this, coupled with the gospel music, seems to suggest a religious theme, it is left so undeveloped that it remains largely irrelevant. That the outer world reaches the room only through shadows, like that revolving shadow of the ambulance that comes to remove Mary Grace, suggests the cave parable from Book VII of Plato's *Republic*. This too is irrelevant.

When Mrs. Turpin leaves the cave-office, the bursts of light she sees are her pigs, luminous at sunset, and the bridge of fire looming over them, bearing a mélange of humankind to heaven. Her heaven, her version of Plato's "Form of Good," is total chaos. Like the echo of Sir Thomas Browne, the fundamentalist gospel music, and Mrs. Turpin's "dialogue" with Jesus, the cave image does little more than provide a suggestion of depth that O'Connor flattens out as the story progresses.

The monumental Mrs. Turpin emerges less through analogies with forms of good than through her obsession with kinds of order. In a sense, the story is a story about structure—about ways of relating the self to the world around it and even of looking into the nature of the self. The structure of the story parallels the structure of life according to Mrs. Turpin. During its rising action she defines herself in relation to others by her greater health and size, then by her possessions, color, and sweet disposition. Its falling action follows an identical order. Mrs. Turpin, fallen from her chair, seems the smallest person in the room, and must look up to everyone there. Her neat farmhouse, her prize possession, seems unreal. She turns to her Negroes for support but cannot believe the sympathy they provide, knowing her color may make it possible to demand sympathy from them but is not enough to bring her genuine warmth. Her belief in herself as a kindly, respectable, Christian woman, shaken by Mary Grace's accusation that she is more wart hog than lady, ends in a realization that her virtues are meaningless.

Mrs. Turpin begins the story by entering the waiting room like "a living demonstration that the room was inadequate and ridiculous" (E, 191). As if to emphasize her hugeness and robustness, she is contrasted with an indolent child slouched in his seat and motionless except for his runny nose. She orders her husband to sit down because of his weak leg and remains standing, looking down on everyone. She alone seems powerful: Claud cannot stand because of the ulcer on his leg, the white-trash family looks sickly and underfed, the old man is asleep, dead, or pretending to be either. The world of the story is the manless society of much of O'Connor's work where men are either old, asleep, dead, diseased, or mutilated, or murderers and thieves. Even the doctor, who emerges in time to calm down Mary Grace, is only pretending to be strong as he speaks in the desperately "off-hand voice young doctors adopt for terrible occasions" (E, 207).

As Joy-Hulga in "Good Country People" wears a shirt with a cowboy on horseback painted on it, so Mary Grace wears the clothes of puberty well into womanhood. Mrs. Turpin and Mary Grace's mother are those familiarly bland, affable, complacent mothers that fill O'Connor's South. Like Joy-Hulga's mother, Mrs. Hopewell, they have no vices themselves but know how to manipulate the defects of other people to their own advantage. In the intimacy that develops between the two older women, Mrs. Turpin takes advantage of the anger between Mary Grace and her mother to aggrandize herself, using the girl's ugliness and contempt as butts for her "good humor." Goaded on by Mary Grace's own mother, she uses Mrs. Chestny's most effective weapons: complacency and pity. The gospel music that filters in through the radio describes the happiest relation to life Mrs. Turpin can achieve: "When I looked up and He looked down. . . ." Mrs. Turpin knows the old song and completes it "Wona these days I know I'll we—eara crown."

Mrs. Turpin literally looks down on everyone. "Without appearing to, Mrs. Turpin always noticed people's feet." She ranks the people in the office according to their shoes, creating another criteria of social class in her obsession to place herself a rung above as many as she can, or, more charitably, to feel as though there is some kind of order in the world. Mrs. Turpin is happy that her good black patent leather shoes outshine the ugly Girl Scout shoes worn by Mary Grace. Appropriately, the white-trash woman wears bedroom slippers to indicate her laziness. Unable to stop herself from thinking about whom to look up to and whom to look down on, Mrs. Turpin is

confused about who could be above her. She becomes so
perplexed about the design of the social world that it ends
by forming no design at all. Her most intense considera-
tions of order end in total chaos. "Usually by the time she
had fallen asleep all the classes of people were moiling and
roiling around in her head, and she would dream they were
all crammed in together in a box car, being ridden off to be
put in a gas oven" (E, 196). Death is the only thing that
can resolve the chaos of society. What ultimately joins
people together is their common mortality, a universal ani-
mality that makes it possible for everyone to be shipped off
like cattle to die. Everyone, the image suggests, is a Jew, a
symbolic alien on his way to a concentration camp to wait
for death.

Mary Grace's wrath grows more fiery as she listens to
her mother using Mrs. Turpin to attack her. O'Connor describes this girl whose face is seared with pimples, whose
eyes smoulder and blaze and show an unnatural light, as an
embodiment of fire, a living image of the fiery apocalypse
she suggests at the end of the story. When Mary Grace
grimaces with disgust at her mother's cliché, "it takes all
kinds to make a world," Mrs. Turpin takes her look as a
personal attack. The cliché turns on Mrs. Turpin's obsession about what kinds of people there are and how they
are arranged to make the world. Mrs. Turpin seems to feel
that Mary Grace does not consider her particularly essential to the social order and feels the girl "was looking at her
as if she had known and disliked her all her life—all of
Mrs. Turpin's life, it seemed too, not just all the girl's life"
(E, 201).

But Mary Grace's greatest fury emerges during a remarkable discussion of what can be done with the South's
alternately exploited and unwanted aliens: the Negroes.
Her exchange of glances with Mrs. Turpin occurs during

a discussion of what should be done with "them." The white-trash woman feels they should be sent back to Africa, while Mrs. Turpin and Mary Grace's mother insist they could never do without their Negro friends. The alternative is to permit them to go to New York and "marry white folks so they can improve their color." Claud remarks that this produces "white-faced niggers." Claud's "joke" leaves Mary Grace bound up in fury as she grips her book with "white fingers." Mary Grace clearly sees herself as a "white-faced nigger"—as a despised alien, an embodiment of what all these people consider least desirable, most ugly, and most frightening. Like Julian, she feels that she too is the slave and victim of "good" women like her mother and Mrs. Turpin.

The joke everyone else finds so funny, like the cliché Mrs. Turpin approves of, turns upon the problem of knowing what one is. Suggesting a mixture like Joe Christmas of Faulkner's *Light in August*, it suggests as well the problem of the dual nature of man, a question that plagues Mrs. Turpin, who cannot understand how she can be both herself and a wart hog, how she can be saved and from hell too.

In one sense, the dual nature of man may be seen in a traditional, religious sense as the gap between the body and soul. Yet this is less relevant in the story than the gap between one's self and one's self-image, a gap that appears objectively in the use of doubles. As the stylish mother of Mary Grace is Mrs. Turpin's ideal self-image, so her daughter—fat, ugly, unpleasant, and disliked, is everything Mrs. Turpin fears becoming. The biggest bribe even Jesus could offer her to turn her from her irrepressible good nature is to make her "svelte and stylish." Hence Mrs. Turpin is not bothered by the irritating white-trash woman but is profoundly bothered by the girl, by her negative self-image. For Mrs. Turpin is named from *tur-pare*—to soil, defile or pollute, and seems to feel dirty herself. She takes refuge in the laughter that follows her husband's joke that has been funny enough to raise the dead, for even the old man laughs. A chorus from the radio sings:

> You go to blank blank
> And I'll go to mine
> But we'll all blank along
> to-geth-ther,
> And all along the blank
> We'll hep eachother out
> Smile-ling in any kind of
> Weath-ther! [E, 202]

Mrs. Turpin "didn't catch every word but she caught enough to agree with the spirit of the song and it turned her thoughts sober" (E, 202). She thinks it is a song about doing good, but it is also a song about nothingness, about "blanking" along through life. The song initiates a stream of thoughts about herself and her own decency that culminates in Mary Grace's giving her the crown she is sure she will one day get from Jesus. She is, in a way, crowned by Mary Grace, given a bruise as a sign of being marked by *Human Development*.

When Mrs. Turpin cries "Oh Jesus, thank you!" Mary hurls her book at her, calls her a wart hog and tells her to go back to hell. For Mary Grace, Mrs. Turpin is the mother she can attack, the one she does not fear to destroy. She tries to strangle her, suffocate her, administer to her the fate of those whom Mrs. Turpin herds into a cattle car in her dream. Her blow knocks all of Mrs. Turpin's props from under her: Mrs. Turpin's spiritual demise begins as she falls from her chair. Mrs. Turpin falls from a world of debased pieties into a more neutral, more frightening world of machines.

Unable to enlarge herself or to magnify her own virtue and goodness, she sees everything through the reverse side of a telescope as shrunken, distant, and immeasurably smaller than before. As Claud's face crumples, even the white-trash woman looks down on her. Mrs. Turpin begins to feel empty, "like a great empty drum of flesh with a heart swinging back and forth in it." She seems to have become a bell or clock or a mere shell that, like a coffin, contains some remnant of life. The image may be one for time and mutability, for life swinging between the poles of redemption and damnation, or one of life as a Christian lady and life as a wart hog. In the context of her ruminations on order, it is an image of chaos, of fluctuating self-esteem, of her inability to find some design in society. She attempts to call Claud but cannot reach him. She feels "like someone trying to catch a train in a dream, when everything moves in slow motion and the faster you try to run the slower you go" (E, 207).

Claud is the train in her dream, a vehicle that will carry her back to normalcy. Her sudden dependency on her husband seems to parallel Mary Grace's collapse. As Mary Grace's eyes burn with pleasure that her message has been heard, she collapses into her mother's lap. "The girl's fingers were gripped like a baby's around her thumb" (E, 208). At the core of Mary Grace's contempt for the human development of Mrs. Turpin there lies some contempt for her own. As Mrs. Turpin's bruised windpipe displays "moon shaped lines like pink fish bones," suggesting the very beginning of human evolution, so Mary

Grace reverts to her own infancy after the oblique attack she has made on her own mother. While the white-trash woman looks down on the girl, whose mother remains on the floor, Mrs. Turpin, like Hazel Motes, Mrs. May, and so many of O'Connor's heroes, has her first view of nothingness as she looks toward her future "straight ahead at nothing." Everything collapses into a blurry, unreal world. The ambulance, "rather the shadow of the ambulance," takes Mary Grace away. Even Mrs. Turpin's possessions seem so insubstantial that she would not be surprised if her prim farm house were "a burnt wound between two blackened chimneys" (E, 209). The familiar human world has receded into the distance with Mary Grace's accusation. Lying on the floor in the doctor's office, she resents being patted like an animal. When she gets home and lies down, lying on her back instantly evokes the image of a razor-backed hog with warts on its face and horns coming out behind its ears. In a sense, she becomes what Mary Grace says she is, an animal. Lying in her bed, she sees unintelligible writing on the ceiling. Unlike the writing the prophet Daniel deciphered, what she sees may be Mary Grace's words, which, like the rest of the human world, have become mysterious and remote. Mrs. Turpin in her metamorphosis grows as illiterate as any other hog as she becomes less human.

After trying to deny that she is a wart hog, and seeking reassurance in her Negroes, she feels still worse. A Negro woman asks her if she fell, perhaps playing on her metaphoric fall from all her props. Her bruise, her crown, begins to look like a tornado about to engulf her brow as she marches toward her pig parlor for a confrontation. Gazing intently on her pigs, she sees herself in an old squinting sow. She begins thinking about her pigs in a way that parallels her thoughts on social class, creating a hierarchy of pigs with a pig astronaut at the top. The pig who became an astronaut is so like a human, so able to maintain a human posture that he dies because he is surrounded by scientists and doctors who forget that he is a pig. He dies because he is left in the posture of a man when he should be on all fours like any hog.

Looking as if she had swallowed a mad dog, Mrs. Turpin hoses down her pigs. She will let none of them lie down, hosing their hind quarters mercilessly, and, in mounting anger, squirting the hose in the eye of her double, the old sow. She blinds the old hog with water, demanding, "How am I a pig and me too? How am I saved and from Hell too?" She becomes so engrossed in her own fury that she cannot hear the pig's squeals of anguish. She herself, in effect, cannot hear her own fury, which she will not express except in a "low fierce voice, barely above a whisper." The sun shines over the pig parlor like a "farmer inspecting his own hogs" (E, 215). And as pigs to an acquisitive farmer is Mrs. Turpin to the gods; they use her for their image of human value.

In her anger at God, she says he could have made her a "nigger" or "trash." "Niggers" and "trash" behave like hogs—they are filthy, lie in the middle of the road, roll on the ground. With her hose, she has tried to stop pigs from being pigs, tried to keep them standing. While the landscape around her pig parlor takes on the colors of her bruise, glassy green and lavender, she screams over it her last assertion of order and rectitude. "Call me a wart hog from hell. Put that bottom rail on the top. There'll still be a top and bottom." Her words rebound from the bruised fields in a garbled echo, as though something insolent in nature mangles every attempt at human order. Her final

plea to Mary Grace, "Who do you think you are?" is
answered immediately with an image:

A tiny truck, Claud's, appeared on the highway, heading
rapidly out of sight. Its gears scraped thinly. It looked like
a child's toy. At any moment a bigger truck might smash
into it and scatter Claud's and the nigger's brains all over
the road [E, 217]

An image of the fragility of both men and machines, it
says, in effect, there is no difference between metal, flesh,
the brains of a nigger or Claud's. The truck of an adult
farmer is like a child's toy, easily crushed, living in the
shadow of destruction by some larger force. The perception that all life, both organic and inorganic, is equally
vulnerable passes immediately into a statement that, if life
means nothing enduring, it must be worth nothing. The
only value seems to exist in destruction, in hurling *Human
Development* at someone and, ultimately, at the floor.

Lacking transcendent qualities Himself, O'Connor's
God lives in a heaven that is very much like the world—
whether imaged as waiting room or hog parlor.[6] When
Mrs. Turpin, who has tried to figure out how she is saved
and from hell too sees heaven from her pig parlor,

She saw the streak as a vast swinging bridge extending up-
ward from the earth through a field of living fire. Upon it
a vast horde of souls were rumbling toward heaven. There
were whole companies of white-trash, clean for the first
time in their lives, and bands of black niggers in white
robes, and battalions of freaks and lunatics shouting and
clapping and leaping like frogs. And bringing up the end
of the procession was a tribe of people whom she recog-
nized at once as those who, like herself and Claud, had always had a little of everything and the God-given wit to
use it right. . . . They were marching behind the others

with great dignity, accountable as they had always been for good order and common sense and respectable behavior. . . . They alone were on key. Yet she could see by their shocked and altered faces that even their virtues were being burned away. She lowered her hands and gripped the rail of the hog pen, her eyes small but fixed unblinkingly on what lay ahead [E, 217-218].

Perhaps Mrs. Turpin is both saved and from hell because damnation and redemption are so alike.[7] As she has her vision of heaven, she grows piglike until, with her small unblinking eyes, she stands immobilized by the hog pen. The sight of heaven destroys her faith in her spiritual qualities and, forcing her back into her body, makes her acknowledge that she is a pig.

Everyone—freaks, lunatics, and even the kindly and respectable, O'Connor's particular *bétes noires*—goes to heaven. Even salvation is a force for leveling all human distinctions. Her heaven is a celebration of violence, a universal chaos in which everything is destroyed. The battalion of freaks and lunatics that alone leaps happily toward it is that same procession of heroes that runs through O'Connor's red clay hills bearing their mania and deformity as signs of the grace of God. Rejoicing in their triumphs over the kind and the loving, she displays her scarred, beloved offspring with a pride fierce and stern as the pride of an ugly woman.

5

What Makes Her "Different":

Flannery O'Connor & Southern Literature

W HILE FLANNERY O'CONNOR was by any standard Southern, perhaps even a Southern lady, in a literary sense she is
that and something more. She saw with alarm that the
South was becoming less "Southern," was "losing its many
faults and few virtues," but she never saw how much she
herself would contribute to the very process of change she
condemned.

Flannery O'Connor instinctively abandoned the traditional concerns of Southern fiction for her own peculiar
obsessions, obsessions which sprang from the unique circumstances of her life. Perhaps quite by chance, those
peculiar concerns cut to the center of the American consciousness and brought her fiction into the mainstream of
American literature. She would use the trappings of Southern life, but make them explode in new and unexpected
directions. When her work is compared to such Southern
contemporaries as William Faulkner, William Styron, and
Truman Capote, its distinctive qualities become clear.

Those habitués of Southern fiction, the one-horse
farmer, the outlaw, the peddler, the itinerant workman,
and the black appear in the work of all four writers. Like
other Southerners, they write about fundamentalist reli-

gion, display that distrust of intellect and abstraction claimed for the South by Robert Penn Warren, and show a world with violent contrasts filled with men doing violence to each other and to the land. Those animals, pecans, chicken coops, and trees that have become the furniture of postbellum Southern fiction can be found in the work of all four authors. Here the resemblances end. Faulkner and Styron build their work on a different scale from O'Connor and Capote. Writing about man mythologizing himself, Faulkner and Styron give the least of his acts the greatest magnitude. The humblest of Faulkner's creations, that idiot Isaac Snopes in *The Hamlet* who falls so passionately in love with his cow, achieves a depth of feeling no one in O'Connor's work ever reaches. Popeye and Temple Drake, whose closest analogue in O'Connor's work is the wooden Sarah Ham of "The Comforts of Home," pursue their sexual violence with such pleasure and devotion that their sordidness achieves a cosmic stature, far exceeding the capacity of O'Connor's heroes, who find "it's no real pleasure in life." Styron's Nat Turner, like so many of the violent heroes of Southern fiction, from William Gilmore Simms's Guy Rivers through Bayard Sartoris, is a romantic transcending himself in his acts, mythologizing them even as he performs them. Like Joe Christmas of *Light in August*, Turner is an American Manfred, a Byronic hero of the Southern backwoods. Both Faulkner and Styron write poems about violence in which action disappears into lyricism, into the legend it creates.

Both O'Connor and the mature Capote write about a world without myths. Even ultimate acts have no power to suggest that feeling of meaning, that sense of overpowering significance that legends are made of. While Styron and Faulkner expand the dimensions of reality, O'Connor and Capote reduce or reflect them. The difference in the scale of life becomes particularly apparent if we compare their attitudes toward those Southern obsessions, the historical past, one's personal ancestry, and the nature of violence. Since all these preoccupations converge in the ultimate act of violence, I have chosen five murder scenes which I feel illustrate the essential gulf between Flannery O'Connor and the more traditional literary South.

O'Connor's fiction lacks that sense of the interpenetration of the past and present that such a traditionalist as Allen Tate considers essential to the writer with a sense of his homeland. The present and the past do not merge in her work but confront each other like monoliths. Where Faulkner could say, "The past is never dead. It is not even past," O'Connor's characters emerge almost historyless from the backwoods with no sense of the historical past and little of their own. While old Tarwater, in *The Violent Bear It Away*, does compare his unwilling stay in a mental hospital to Jonah's sojourn in the whale, or Ezekiel's stay in the pit, he never transforms the reality of his hospitalization, never goes beyond a literal comparison of himself to the old prophets and never moves from metaphor to myth. In contrast, Virginia Du Pre's account of Bayard Sartoris's death before the second battle of Manassas is a great human triumph over the real, the banal, the senseless:

> . . . as she grew older the tale itself grew richer and richer, taking on a mellow splendor like wine; until what had been a hare-brained prank of two heedless and reckless boys wild with their own youth had become a gallant and finely tragical focal point to which the history of the race had been raised from out the old miasmic swamps of spiritual sloth by two angels valiantly fallen and strayed, altering the course of human events and purging the souls of men.[1]

There is no comparable sense of the honor or grandeur of the antebellum South in O'Connor's fiction. The South before and during the Civil War emerges only in such echoes as the search for the mansion in "A Good Man Is Hard to Find" and Julian's lament for the Godhigh mansion in "Everything That Rises Must Converge." Looking for the past in the former results in a mass murder and, in the latter, in the squelching of Julian's independence and manhood. The antebellum Southern past does not exist as a standard of value, or even as an index of what has been lost, a tape measure of how life has fallen. It exists as a fiction for the aged and infantile.

The absence of a social or personal sense of history in O'Connor's fiction becomes still more striking when we compare her image of man at the last moment of his own history, or at the moment when he ends the history of another, with similar images in Faulkner, Styron, and Capote. All involve heroes as alienated as O'Connor's, all men who are Misfits and from whose acts similar themes emerge. I have chosen Percy Grimm's murder of Joe Christmas in *Light in August*, Nat Turner's murder of Margaret in *The Confessions of Nat Turner*, the Misfit's murder of the grandmother in "A Good Man is Hard to Find," Hazel Motes's murder of Solace Layfield in *Wise Blood*, and Perry Smith's and Richard Hickock's murder of Mr. Clutter and his daughter, Nancy, in *In Cold Blood*.

In *Light in August*, Grimm, moved by an inexorable Player,

> ran straight to the kitchen . . . already firing, almost before he could have seen the table overturned and standing on its edge across the corner of the room, and the bright and glittering hands of the men who crouched behind it, resting upon the upper edge. Grimm emptied the automatic's magazine into the table; later someone covered all five shots with a folded handkerchief. . . . When the others reached the kitchen they saw the table flung aside now and Grimm

stooping over the body. When they approached to see what he was about, they saw that the man was not dead yet, and when they saw what Grimm was doing one of the men gave a choked cry and stumbled back into the wall and began to vomit. Then Grimm too sprang back, flinging behind him the bloody butcher knife. "Now you'll let white women alone, even in hell," he said. He just lay there, with his eyes open and empty of everything save consciousness, and with something, a shadow, about his mouth. For a long moment he looked up at them with peaceful and unfathomable and unbearable eyes. Then his face, body, all, seemed to collapse, to fall in upon itself, and from out the slashed garments about his hips and loins the pent black blood seemed to rush like a released breath. It seemed to rush out of his pale body like the rush of sparks from a rising rocket; upon that black blast the man seemed to rise soaring into their memories forever and ever. They are not to lose it, in whatever peaceful valleys, beside whatever placid and reassuring streams of old age, in the mirroring faces of whatever children they will contemplate old disasters and newer hopes. It will be there, musing quiet, steadfast, not fading and not particularly threatful, but of itself alone serene, of itself triumphant. Again from the town, deadened a little by the walls, the scream of the siren mounted toward its unbelievable crescendo, passing out of the realm of hearing.[2]

In *The Confessions of Nat Turner* Nat raises the sword that hangs in his right hand "like the weight of all the earth" to kill Margaret. When he strikes the first blow, he says,

I heard for the first time her hurtful, ragged breathing, and it was with this sound in my ears that I plunged the sword into her side, just below and behind her breast. She screamed then at last. Litheness, grace—all fled her like ghosts. She crumpled to earth, limp, a rag, and as she fell I stabbed her again in the same place, or near it, where pulsing blood already encrimsoned the taffeta's blue. There was no scream this time although the echo of the first sang in my ears like a far angelic cry; when I turned aside from her fallen body I was troubled by a steady soughing noise like the rise and fall of a summer tempest in a grove of pines and realized that it was the clamor of my own breathing as it welled up in sobs in my chest.

I lurched away from her through the field, calling out to myself like one bereft of mind. Yet hardly had I taken a dozen steps when I heard her voice, weak, frail, almost without breath, not so much voice as memory—faint as if from some distant and half-forgotten lawn of childhood: Oh Nat I hurt so. Please kill me Nat I hurt so.

I stopped and looked back. "Die. God damn your white soul," I wept. "Die!"

Oh Nat please kill me I hurt so.

"Die! Die! Die! Die!"

The sword fell from my hand. I returned to her side and looked down. Her head was cradled against the inside of her arm, as if she had composed herself for sleep, and all the chestnut streaming luxuriance of her hair had fallen in a tangle amid the hayfield's parched and fading green. Grasshoppers stitched and stirred in restless fidget among the weeds, darting about her face.

"I hurt so," I heard her whisper.

"Shut your eyes," I said. I reached down to search with my fingers for a firm length of fence rail and I could sense once more her close girl-smell and the fragrance of lavender, bitter in my nostrils and sweet. "Shut your eyes," I told her quickly. Then when I raised the rail above her head she gazed at me, as if past the imponderable vista of her anguish, with a grave and drowsy tenderness such as I had never known, spoke some words too soft to hear, and, saying no more, closed her eyes upon all madness, illusion, error, dream, and strife. So I brought the timber down and she was swiftly gone, and I hurled the hateful, shattered club far up into the weeds.

For how long I aimlessly circled her body—prowled around the corners of the field in haphazard quest for nothing like some roaming dog—how long this went on I do not recollect.[3]

In *Wise Blood*, when Hazel Motes wreaks his vengeance on Solace Layfield,

The Prophet began to run in earnest. He tore off his shirt and unbuckled his belt and ran out of the trousers. He began grabbing for his feet as if he would take off his shoes too, but before he could get at them, the Essex knocked him flat and ran over him. Haze drove about twenty feet and stopped the car and then began to back it. He backed it over the body and then stopped and got out. The Essex stood half over the other Prophet as if it were pleased to guard what it had finally brought down. The man didn't look so much like Haze, lying on the ground on his face without his hat or suit on. A lot of blood was coming out of him and forming a puddle around his head. He was motionless all but for one finger that moved up and down in front of his face as if he were marking time with it. Haze poked his toe in his side and he wheezed for a second and then was quiet. "Two things I can't stand," Haze said, "a man that ain't true and one that mocks what is. You shouldn't never have tampered with me if you didn't want what you got."

. . . "Told where [my daddy's] still was and got five dollars for it," the man gasped.

"You shut up now," Haze said.

"Jesus hep me," the man wheezed. Haze gave him a hard slap on the back and he was quiet. He leaned down to hear if he was going to say anything else but he wasn't breathing any more. Haze turned around and examined the front of the Essex to see if there had been any damage done to it.

The bumper had a few splurts of blood on it but that was all. Before he turned around and drove back to town, he wiped them off with a rag. [W, 204-205]

In his conversation with the grandmother in "A Good Man Is Hard to Find" the Misfit becomes upset because he does not know whether Christ raised the dead. The grandmother says,

> "Why you're one of my babies. You're one of my own children!" She reached out and touched him on the shoulder. The Misfit sprang back as if a snake had bitten him and shot her three times through the chest. Then he put his gun down on the ground and took off his glasses and began to clean them.
>
> Hiram and Bobby Lee returned from the woods and stood over the ditch, looking down at the grandmother who half sat and half lay in a puddle of blood with her legs crossed under her like a child's and her face smiling up at the cloudless sky.
>
> Without his glasses, the Misfit's eyes were red-rimmed, and pale and defenseless-looking. "Take her off and throw her where you thrown the others," he said, picking up the cat that was rubbing itself against his leg.
>
> "She was a talker, wasn't she?" Bobby Lee said, sliding down the ditch with a yodel.
>
> "She would of been a good woman," the Misfit said, "if it had been somebody there to shoot her every minute of her life."
>
> "Some fun!" Bobby Lee said.
>
> "Shut up, Bobby Lee," the Misfit said. "It's no real pleasure in life." [G, 28-29]

In Truman Capote's *In Cold Blood* Perry Smith describes the murders of Mr. Clutter and his daughter, Nancy:

> ... I roped her feet together and tied her hands behind her back. Then I pulled up the covers, tucked her in till just

her head showed. There was a little easy chair near the bed, and I thought I'd rest a minute; my legs were on fire—all that climbing and kneeling. I asked Nancy if she had a boy friend. She said yes, she did. She was trying hard to act casual and friendly. I really liked her. She was really nice. A very pretty girl and not spoiled or anything. She told me quite a lot about herself. About school and how she was going to a university to study music and art. Horses. Said next to dancing what she liked best was to gallop a horse, so I mentioned my mother had been a champion rodeo rider. . . . All the time we were talking, we could hear the lunatic roaming around below, looking for the safe. Looking behind pictures. Tapping on the walls. Tap tap tap. Like some nutty woodpecker. . . . I gave the gun to Dick. He took aim, and she turned her face to the wall.

I knelt down beside Mr. Clutter, and the pain of kneeling —I thought of that dollar. Silver dollar. The shame. Disgust. And they'd told me never to come back to Kansas. But I didn't realize what I'd done till I heard the sound. Like somebody drowning. Screaming under water. I handed the knife to Dick. Finish him, you'll feel better. I told Dick to hold the flashlight, focus it. Then I aimed the gun. The room just exploded.

I thought he was a very nice gentleman, [Mr. Clutter] Soft spoken. I thought so right up to the moment I cut his throat.[4]

The murders in Faulkner and Styron tell more how a man makes symbols than how he kills or dies. For Christmas and Turner, murder is a repudiation of slavery, a release from the burden of the South's most peculiar institution and the Negro ancestry that makes them its victims. They have a sense of race as a force of destiny, of fate unfolding in the blood of a man so powerfully that it can only be expressed in murder or escaped in death. For example, Joe Christmas's murder of Joanna Burden frees him from a restrictive society with its "orderly parade of named and numbered days and fence pickets," and lets him lose himself in nature, where he finds some redemption in a world beyond fury or despair. Similarly, he resolves in his own death the ambiguity of his mulatto blood. In the release of his mixed blood he becomes a symbol of composure growing more profound and expansive with time.

In contrast, the murders in O'Connor's and Capote's fiction are murders without creation, murders without mythology. They occur in an historical void with neither feeling nor conviction nor consciousness. The murderer never transcends himself but, like Mrs. Turpin, whose vision of heaven only made her more porcine, he remains so enmeshed in his own body that he cannot see his victim, cannot realize that he is the creator of someone's last sensation. Not in nature nor in the intense, personal confrontation of murder or death can he escape himself. For example, Motes wants to kill Solace Layfield because he is his double, an unpleasant self-image. When Layfield is dying, he finds he does not really resemble him. His murder has not resolved his own self-hatred, nor destroyed what of Layfield is in him. His unsuccessful, partial "suicide" becomes an act of minor resentment not unlike the Misfit's annoyance at being interrupted by the grandmother. Like the Clutter murder described by Perry Smith, it is an almost totally affectless act, a small protrusion on the flat surface of life. It resolves nothing and changes nothing. This becomes clear if we look at the style, the surface of the action, in each of the scenes.

The importance of Joe Christmas's death lies not in its action, not in the detail of the shooting or castration, but in its meaning. The action at the core of the episode is slowed and diminished so that significance flows free.

Faulkner's account moves quickly from a description of Grimm's firing at Christmas, done so carelessly that Grimm fires almost at random, without aiming, to a description of the table that stands between Grimm and his victim. With its five bullet holes to be covered by a folded handkerchief, the table, not Christmas, is emphasized. Had Gavin Stevens not told us earlier that Christmas held Joanna Burden's unfired gun, we could not know from the murder scene what made Christmas's fingers so "bright and glittering." Similarly, we know of the castration "second hand" from its significance to Grimm and to the man who vomits, sickened by it. Since Faulkner does not describe the murder until page 440, but has Gavin Stevens tell us how Joe Christmas was killed on page 314, we know the murder occurs long before we see it. These ruminations before the event both suppress the action of the murder and expand its meaning.

Speculating on Mrs. Hines's effect on her grandson, Christmas, Gavin Stevens builds a kind of mythic frame for the scene. He claims it was more than Percy Grimm, moved by an inexorable Player, who killed him. "It was not alone all those thirty years which she (Mrs. Hines) did not know, but all those successions of thirty years before that which had put that stain either on his white blood or his black blood, whichever you will, and which killed him."[5]

Christmas seems to have been killed by an accumulation of history, by those successions of thirty years that stretch from the present into a remote past beyond his birth toward some origin in a primal taint placed on either his black blood or his white. The stain may be a fusion of the fall of man and the fall of the South; a combination of original sin and of the South's most peculiar institution. Christmas, whose black and white blood are at war, is an embodiment of the chaos caused by the fall. Whether the lament is for the fact of slavery itself or for the loss of a slave society in which the Negro had a stable, fixed place is unclear. The fall from Eden and the fall of the South merge as a general fall into confusion, disunity, and a disorder so great that it fills the blood of men.

The tragedy of Joe Christmas as a man is that he is alien to both white and black society, without a position in either. He is free only in nature, where he can live, *sui generis*, in a totally anomic state. He may be Christlike because his fate is to suffer for the accumulated sins of men, for the crimes of those who first bought slaves, and for the sin of his father, unknown but presumably black and Mexican. From his animal freedom he is recalled only by his grandmother, who, telling him of his origin, reminds him of his connection to humankind. Her reminder precipitates the death that defines his place in society.

In his death, Christmas reaches atonement with his black blood. It "rushes out" like a "relieved breath," a "rush of sparks from a rising rocket," a blast that makes him soar in an orgiastic apotheosis. If no trumpets accompany his flight, it is marked by the sound of the siren, which, transcending itself like Christmas, soars high out of hearing as he soars into the symbol he becomes in memory.

In his sexualized death, as in his affair with Joanna Burden, Christmas is the victim of Southern history. As Grimm is a kind of parody of chivalric devotion to Southern Womanhood, so Joanna Burden parodies the New England reformer. She knows all the rhetoric of empathy and equality but in her career as a "nymphomaniac," remarkable if only for its meteoric rise and fall, never sees him as more than a sexual stereotype. Like any slave-owner of the classic slave-owning school, she will sleep with her darkie but not join him for dinner. Calling him

"Negro!" "Negro!" in her transports, she calls him by all he is to her.

In his murder and death, Christmas is not simultaneously the lover and victim of white society. He chooses to be both its destroyer and its victim. That his victimization extends back beyond his birth makes him also a metaphor for all mortality. After his revenge on Joanna Burden, he never fires his pistol, never protects himself from the onslaught of Grimm, and, in his acceptance of his death he becomes triumphant. Overcoming the ambiguity of his blood, of his life, he becomes an image of unity and atonement. The ambiguous reality of his days soars, in his "apotheosis," into pure symbol, pure significance. He triumphs over time: over the "peaceful valley" (death), "the streams of old age" (Lethean forgetfulness), and the faces of children yet unborn (the future).

Like Joe Christmas, Styron's Nat Turner is an alien estranged from white society and black. Barred from the first by his black skin and from the second by his white learning, he bears the burden of both Southern history and his own ancestry. Merging with the past of his race, his own past blends into an accumulation of horrors which he hopes to revenge in the future. He sees the blood he will shed as a way of transcending his servitude, a way of redeeming himself as a man, and of defining himself in a new way in white society. His violence is meant as a gesture of denial, a repudiation of the white South. Like Christmas's murder of Joanna Burden, it has an unexpected result. Like Grimm's murder of Christmas, it ends in the creation of a symbol and in the apotheosis of the victim. More fortunate than Grimm, Nat too transcends himself in the act. As Margaret becomes an angel, speaking with an angel's cry, he becomes compassionate.

As Faulkner scrambled the sequence of time in *Light in*

August, so Styron uses devices that let time evolve as *durée,* as significant action. Styron has Turner, a historical figure of the nineteenth century, describe a murder committed in a past before the book begins, recall acts summoned from his earliest years, and filtered through his memory. The action has so meshed with its significance to him that the murder has a magical, lyrical quality, more idyllic than gory. As Gavin Stevens tells us what happened to Christmas before we see it, so Styron anticipates the murder in an earlier scene when, as he is driving along a deserted road with Margaret, she sees an injured turtle and wants him to stop so they can help it. In response to her sympathy he says, "Ain't nothing but a turtle, Missy," and kicks it with his toe. When she persists, he kills it with a hickory stick, throwing the stick into the field. "Twasn't nothing but an old turtle Missy.... Turtles don't feel anything.... They's an old nigger sayin' about animals that goes, 'They that doesn't holler, doesn't hurt.' "[6] The episode leaves him sexually aroused, thinking "Never could I remember having been so unhinged by desire and hatred."[7] His murder scene, preluded by "Ah how I want her," resolves the conflict of desire and hatred, and answers the question implicit in both scenes: Should a Negro slave feel pity for a turtle or a white Southern woman?

That he so obviously desires her sexually throughout her appearance in the book and neither rapes her nor is hostile toward her in a sexual way is striking. It may be his love for her, that confused inchoate tenderness that seems so much a part of his sexual feeling for her, that keeps him from raping her. His desire is so mingled with yearning and love that it seems easier for him to kill her as a symbol of White Womanhood than to face the mixture of tenderness and hatred she arouses. His tenderness and compassion are only freed when she is dying. After she becomes an angel, a memory and not a voice, she is no longer sexually attainable, no longer a threat to the life he has chosen. Like Grimm's murder of Christmas, Nat's begins with an account of its trappings. Nat's awareness of her body emerges in the visual imagery of her blue dress stained with red blood. After he stabs her, the passage moves from a description of her to one of her effect on him, her merging into nature, and his "madness" and eventual animalization into a "roaming dog." When her voice becomes an angelic cry he becomes aware of his own sobs, his own feeling, and then moves into the fields like "one bereft of mind." He hears her ask for death not as a voice, but as a memory, as something remote. He attempts to stereotype her, as Joanna Burden did Christmas, saying, "Damn your white soul, die!" Her body and its significance to him begin to diverge. Her whiteness becomes secondary, unimportant. Her meaning floats away from her body as he finds that she cannot be depersonalized as an emblem of white womanhood. She becomes instead a symbol of human suffering. Her hair tangling with the grass, her face brushed by grasshoppers, she seems a part of nature. She forces him to feel for her what she felt for the turtle, teaches him compassion—something as bitter to him as the scent of her lavender. She transcends her anguish in a grave and drowsy tenderness. The club which both redeems and destroys her is the instrument of his murder and compassion.

He circles her body to enclose the episode, to seal it off from the life he has chosen for himself. The compassion she has aroused has no place in a life of vengeance. As Christmas's death triumphed over time, so Styron's episode lives beyond the limits of its action. In circling Margaret's body, in trying to encapsulate the episode, Nat seals it off from the rest of his life, letting it float, like the image of the white marble temple that begins and ends the book, in a timeless substance of fantasy.

If Christmas dies because he is reminded of his birth and connection to the white world, Turner dies because Margaret makes him feel compassion. What kills him is the tenderness she aroused, the compassion that made him, after killing her, spare another young girl fleeing from his band through the fields to betray his presence to the countryside.

Both Turner and Christmas become Christs, albeit of a different sort, dying because of their involvement with the white world. Christmas defines himself as a Negro by becoming a supreme victim, choosing to die without defending himself. Turner, taught compassion by a white woman, in a dim unconscious way tries to atone for his act by sparing another girl and goes to his death—if not regretful of his leadership—forgiving her for her whiteness and regretting her death. Perhaps their death suggests only that both *Light in August* and *The Confession of Nat Turner* were written by white Southern Christians who cannot help but associate the dignity of the Negro with his suffering, with his acceptance of his fate, and with his compassion for his oppressor.

What is more relevant is that both Faulkner and Styron have written fundamentally Christian books using the themes of the fall of man and the fall of the South almost interchangeably and the crucifixion, the image of the dying, triumphant god in a general way to express the dignity of human life, its strength and endurance. They write within a framework of traditional meaning, with a strong sense of the gradations of value in life. What endures in their work are the values that endured in the world of Lear: the power of the human flesh, the immensity of passion, the ability to survive a cataclysmic confusion and to emerge with a peace more profound. The image of Lear roaming aged and half mad on the heath looms behind those unaccommodated men of Faulkner, behind Turner roaming in his field, or Christmas, half animal in the Southern backwoods. All are great romantic, mythic figures living always on the pinnacles of meaning. At the core of Faulkner's world are men like Sutpen, Christmas, and Benjy Compson—giants radiating a feeling of immense significance though they may be dead when the story is told, unintrospective animal men, idiots who yet retain an immense sensitivity to nature and to love. Those monumental women, Dilsey, Lena Grove, and Eula Varner are equally huge, half real and half symbol.

While, from a statistical point of view considering annual income, national origin, and religion, some of O'Connor's heroes could wander into Yoknapatawpha, one senses they would find it totally alien. Faulkner and Styron build their countries out of the South's greatest literary virtue: its ability to lag behind the rest of America in giving up the romantic sense of the hero and of history. O'Connor and Capote have abandoned the South's most distinctive concerns. Whether by choice or default, they write out of the mainstream of the American consciousness. In their murder scenes, a framework of meaning, if it exists at all, has receded into so remote a distance that it provides no scale of value. While Christmas and Turner transcend a life of ambivalence and ambiguity, make of their murders and death a resolution of significance to them and to us, the fate of the Misfit and Motes, of Smith and Hickock, remains irrelevant in a larger sense, even to them.

Smith, Motes, and the Misfit can connect nothing with nothing. They are so estranged from themselves, so out of touch with their own feelings that they only know them from external signs or infer them from their own actions. Like the Misfit who speaks most honestly with his gun, or Motes, whose most potent part is his car, they come closest to connecting with objects, things which magically fulfill their fantasies of destruction. Looming about O'Connor's vivid acts of violence is an immense and total silence. It is the silence that engulfs the Misfit's polite speech as he shoots the grandmother. It is in this silence that Flannery O'Connor becomes most eloquent. Like a painter with a genius for using negative space, O'Connor says most about human feeling when she says nothing. In both her murder scenes it is what is left out that says most.

O'Connor clearly intended "A Good Man Is Hard to Find" to *be* tragedy and *Wise Blood* to burlesque it. But the two are oddly alike. Missing in both is a sense of human death, human life or directly felt passion. Both the story and novel convey a feeling of undifferentiated life—of there being few distinctions between living and dying. O'Connor conveys a sense of consuming meaninglessness. If Faulkner was obsessed with the power of memory, the power that let Virginia Du Pre make myths, O'Connor is obsessed with the power of forgetfulness. As the Misfit observes, "you can do one thing or you can do another, kill a man or take a tire off his car, because sooner or later you're going to forget what it was you done and just be punished for it" (G, 26). He cannot remember his own crime because "they never shown me my papers" (G, 27).

Like Motes's Essex, the Mistfit's papers, kept by the Authorities, would explain why he was imprisoned, would anchor him to reality and give some direction to a mind that gropes to make his crime—which he has forgotten—equal his punishment—which seems to be his life. Although the Misfit thinks a lot about the Authorities and even the miracles of Christ, what he affirms is not the existence or nonexistence of either. He affirms the sameness of all events, the difficulty of telling the difference between murdering a man or stealing his tire. Where the deaths of Christmas and Margaret float endlessly significant, no death has much meaning for the Misfit.

What frees the Misfit from total emptiness is his gun. Solid and enduring in his otherwise blank universe, the gun expresses the Misfit's unfathomable rage. Its "voice" is far more authentic than the polite phrases he uses to address the family before he has them exterminated. The gun is his most "animal" part, a potent extension of himself. When the grandmother touches him, her touch is like a snakebite. And for the first time in this story where he has behaved like the politest of backwoods gentlemen, he answers that snakebite touch with an instinctual, immediate gunshot.

The grandmother's gesture of "tenderness"—her claim that he is one of her babies—is ambiguous and ironic.[8] All her babies that we know of are dead, killed, in a sense, by her own manipulation of their trip and her desire to keep their wills infantile and subjected to her own. In likening him to one of her dead babies, she may be reminding him of his own mortality. Her tenderness diminishes, infantilizes him, minimizing his power as a murderer. Suggesting that he is as helpless as a baby, she implies that she can somehow cure his misery like Asbury's mother in "The Enduring Chill," who convinces her son that she can overpower death. She resembles all those indefatigibly optimistic, powerful mothers in O'Connor's fiction. Sitting in her blood like a smiling child, she seems an earlier Mrs. Chestny who has spent her life looking for the past and reverts to her childhood in death. At a moment when she is surely the Misfit's victim, as Mrs. Chestny was the victim of the Negro woman's "emancipation," she tries to be his redeemer. Like Mrs. Chestny, who tried to put the Negro woman in her place with a bright new penny, the grandmother tries to buy off the Misfit's revenge with a gesture. Like Mrs. Chestny, she is attacked in the heart, shot three times in the chest. Although the Misfit's voice is on the verge of breaking as he laments his absence at the miracles of Christ—perhaps he cries as his red-rimmed eyes imply —he shoots her quickly and, cleaning his glasses, restores his perspective on life as he orders her thrown with the other bodies.

O'Connor probably intended her Misfit hero to be a kind of Christ. But the grandmother who tries to be his mother also tries to be his redeemer, his Christ. Beneath the veneer of kindness and gentility, it is clear that these two Christs are crucifying *each other*. The most powerful crucifixion for O'Connor is the one you live out daily for a lifetime, the constant agony involved in human contact, human needs, and human striving. It is, in large part, the agony of being part of the human chain, of having a grandmother who wants to "care" for you. For O'Connor, it is the horror she sees at the core of family life. Almost predictably, the only one who can survive this family outing is the cat, Pitty Sing, who rubs herself pleasurably against the Misfit's leg.

A cause of the accident and the murders, the cat who jumps when the grandmother moves her knees, jumps at random. The cat is too slender a figure to carry much symbolic weight. The cat's leap is not one that seems the result of an accumulation of history or of a lifetime of mingled hatred and desire. It seems no expression of some ultimate cosmic force. The meaning of the cat seems to derive precisely from its symbolic thinness. That a pet, a cat, leaping at random for no great reason, should cause the destruction of an entire family expresses the randomness, the pointlessness of the murders. That the cat's name is Pitty Sing suggests O'Connor's attitude toward violence. In the *Mikado*, it is Pitti Sing who remarks in a sprightly way, "Well, dear, it can't be denied that the fact that your husband is to be beheaded in a month does seem to take the top off it, you know." It does indeed.

Like O'Connor, Pitti Sing sings without pity, a precursor of doom without human compassion. The murders in "A Good Man Is Hard to Find" are of no particular importance to the cat, or to the Misfit. They are not the stuff romantic legends are made of. Only a cat and a Misfit survive the human wreck as detached observers of the scene.

What endures at the end of "A Good Man Is Hard to Find" are two "animals"—the Misfit, who remembers the suffocation of life in prison and whose response to the snakebite touch of the grandmother is an instinctual bite in return, and the cat, who jumps when her body is disturbed and who rubs herself pleasurably against the murderer of the woman who cared for her. Both are equally involved in their own physical sensations. In Hazel Motes's murder of Solace Layfield in *Wise Blood* the animal world recedes into the background and what emerges is a machine and two mechanical men.

Since Layfield is Motes's double and Motes himself is more an abstraction than a man, the scene shows a caricature killing a parody of itself. Its emotional tone is flattened by the precision with which O'Connor keeps to the details of the murder. We are told how the car goes forward and backward, what remains of Layfield's clothes, how Motes cleans his car: we receive a listing as precise as if the point of the scene were not death but empirical accuracy. Where Faulkner and Styron move from detail to affect, from things to symbols, O'Connor gives us the facts and nothing more. That some details like Layfield's desperate attempt to get out of his Motes costume and inability to get out of his shoes, or the image of a dying man literally marking time with his finger, are faintly comic only further reduces the power of the scene. The pleased automobile, happy to stand guard, is the only one there who has much feeling.

As in Grimm's murder of Christmas, there are some symbolic overtones in the scene. Solace, who took Motes's name in vain, betrayed his father for five dollars when he told the police about his still. He is a kind of Judas who, about to die, decides to make the best of it and confess to Motes, the anti-Christ. Layfield is more matter of fact than evil and Motes listens to his confession in the spirit in which it is made. With Layfield marking time as he confesses, his repentance seems merely another listing of details, a stripping off of an anti-Motes costume that repeats the scene before. As Motes he was an anti-Christ, as anti-Motes a seeker of Jesus. In both costumes he seems to play an elaborate end game while he marks time. Wiping the blood from his Essex, Motes wipes away all trace of Layfield, who is heard of no more. Motes leaves the body without remorse, regret, or even speculation.

That the automobile is the most responsive agent in the murder suggests the affectless, mechanical quality of the act itself. Motes's murder is an act without human involvement. That the flat, farcical quality appears in both O'Connor's murder scenes may suggest her own attitude about the value of human life. While it may be possible to explain the shallowness of the scene in *Wise Blood* as inevitable in a novel declared comic by its author, it is less simple to justify the triumph of the Misfit and Pitty Sing. If O'Connor is less a writer of mythic proportion than Faulkner and Styron, she may be more of a realist. A comparable sense of life occurs in the scene Truman Capote records as a genuine human document.

As the Misfit and Motes are enmeshed in their own sense of pain and spite, Perry Smith is much more aware of the pain in his leg, his disgust with Dick Hickock, and his anger at not finding more money at the Clutters' house than of what he is doing. Occurring in some remote periphery of vision, the murder never really touches consciousness. Smith only knows what he has done when he hears the sound of someone dying and realizes Mr. Clutter is drowning in his own blood. He almost infers that he has cut Clutter's throat from the presence of Clutter dying with his throat cut. Similarly, Motes kills Layfield for being his double and notices, when Layfield is lying in his blood, that he does not resemble him. No longer seeing himself in his double, Motes does not recognize himself in the act. Both he and Smith are remarkably removed from their own actions. As the Misfit's conversation with the grandmother is punctuated by gunshots from the woods, so Smith's talk with Nancy, with its veneer of sanity and politeness, friendship and confidences, is dotted with Hickock's lunatic tapping and culminates in the murder of the woman involved. And the deposition form of Smith's account is not unlike O'Connor's factual description of Motes's crime.

While Faulkner and Styron expand the scale of human passion, and Capote claims to reflect it, O'Connor usually reduces it. O'Connor's heroes are neither human, nor symbolic, nor heroic in any traditional sense. On one level, they are projections of O'Connor's fantasies of revolt; on another they are heroes of our time. O'Connor made fiction out of their emptiness, tragedies out of the ice in their blood. She cut so deep into that ice that she reached the general American tragedy of living in cold blood. This is the tragedy of being totally incapable of tragedy, of pervasive emotional death, of minimal human involvement. In committing herself creatively to characters who have neither soul nor depth, O'Connor made poetry out of the surface of reality.

O'Connor's country is a land where meaning flattens out, where there is no sense of continuity great enough to create a sense of history. It is a world as episodic and as brightly colored as the cartoons she loved to draw. In fact, what springs most vividly from her work are cartoons—flat pictures of things, of reified men, and "animal" heroines like the porcine Mrs. Turpin. O'Connor projected the pathos of life in a picture world in "Parker's Back." Parker is an image of chaos in that story about a man who, tattooing himself with eagles and hearts, emblems of love and war, covered his body with images of his power in both, but try as he might, could never make them form a coherent design. Tattooing on his back a Byzantine Christ, he hopes the power of its suffering will win the love of his contemptuous wife and make, from the scattered pictures on his body, a single form. Yet the portrait he bears on his back does not bring about reunion. It rather caricatures how much his back has already been broken by the abrasions of time and his wife's pervasive rejection. Like Parker himself, Christ can connect nothing with nothing. And Parker's back was cut for nothing. His primitive Christ is no more than a caricature of pointless human suffering, stripped of value, stripped of myth. Etched into his body, those disparate emblems of power, those symbols of love and war in cartoon colors, without coherence or design, express, with a terrible eloquence, life.

Parker writes his biography on his body. For him and for O'Connor, life is precisely a mass of chaotic pictures.

In these clearly labeled "episodes" all of feeling inheres.
O'Connor's characters have no inner life. Nor, in a sense,
do they have a character. Living soullessly and deadly by
their frontal lines and masses, they exist on the surface of
reality, anchoring themselves to life with things—literal
anchors for Parker, a car for Motes, a gun for the Misfit—
or with *pictures* of loving hearts. Genuine feeling always
eludes them. Even if they come alive in some violent and
destructive act, their passion is so muted, or so displaced
onto a double, a mechanical object, or an impersonal force,
that their very violence does not seem to spring from
within. It seems to inhere not in them but in their situation.

O'Connor's impulse toward the concrete reduces all of
human feeling to its visible signs: tattoos, pictures, or
specific actions. O'Connor crushes all of human value at
its source in human passion. She stops meaning at its core,
binds it firmly to the specific and the concrete. For example, where Faulkner and Styron see their black heroes
as embodiments of the force of negritude, a blackness that
is both a mystery unto itself and a power that evokes all
the magical forces of passion and nature, Flannery O'Connor treats her black characters one-dimensionally. For her,
being black is simply another way of being a misfit in
Southern society. The black woman who strikes Mrs.
Chestny is no more than a counterpart of the white Protestant Misfit. For Faulkner and Styron, racial conflict is
no external thing, no open confrontation between victim
and oppressor; it enters the blood of Joe Christmas and
the mind of Nat Turner and forces them to war against
themselves. For Flannery O'Connor, racial conflict is a
spectacle: a tableau of a black woman hitting a Mrs.
Chestny. It is a beautifully wrought cartoon with no "insides." O'Connor's is an art of raw power without depth.
It has all the force of a series of expletives strung together

with great intensity; a sequence of episodes that spontaneously explode, erupt without human guidance or a human source.

O'Connor's heroes live without a sense of history and with little connection to their own past. The Misfit and Motes spring out of nowhere to murder. Their most violent acts consume themselves, die when they end, and leave no mark on anyone's consciousness. O'Connor's world has lost its symbols. It is filled with objects and acts which become signs of what things might mean, if they had significance, or what men might feel, if they felt at all. Her reductive, leveling impulse may be part of the demythologizing process in American fiction, a process usually associated with Northerners like William Carlos Williams or the more urbane Wallace Stevens. The career of O'Connor's fellow Southerner, Capote, from his neo-gothic *Other Voices, Other Rooms* through *In Cold Blood* may indicate a similar process in Southern fiction. That both an avowed Catholic and a purveyor of rococo fantasies should be fascinated by the meaningless violence of men flat as the Kansas prairies may show that Southern literature is becoming as "Americanized" as the economy of Atlanta. But it is impossible to say for sure whether O'Connor's work anticipated or foretold the sensibility that would create *In Cold Blood*, or whether it suggests the direction Southern fiction will take in the future.

What we can know for sure is that Flannery O'Connor created a remarkable art, unique in its time. Unlike any Southern writer before her, she wrote in praise of ice in the blood. She celebrated the emotional death that freed her psychic freaks from an agony of human needs, human ties, and human longings. As Parker would never have to see the image of his suffering cut into his *back*, so O'Connor would prevent all her heroes from having to come face to face with their own agonizing rage. If they never found joy in their estrangement from their own feeling, they found an ignorance of themselves that was the closest they could come to bliss. O'Connor took from them memory, the inner life that would have engulfed them in guilt or fear. She helped them fulfill all their dreams of revenge or revolt. She let them live on the surface of life without pleasure or remorse. She left them, to change a Georgia phrase, just as happy as dead hogs lying in the road.

Selected Bibliography

ALICE, Rose, Sister, S.S.J. "Flannery O'Connor: Poet to the Outcast," *Renascence*, XVI (Winter 1964), 126-132.

BARTHES, Roland. "Objective Literature: Alain Robbe-Grillet," in *Two Novels by Robbe-Grillet* (New York, 1965), 11-27.

BASSAN, Maurice. "Flannery O'Connor's Way: Shock With Moral Intent," *Renascence*, XV (Summer 1963), 195-199, 211.

BAUMBACH, Jonathan. "The Acid of God's Grace: The Fiction of Flannery O'Connor," *Georgia Review*, XVII (Fall 1963), 334-346.

BRITTAIN, Joan. "The Fictional Family of Flannery O'Connor," *Renascence*, XIX (Summer 1967), 48-52.

BURKE, John J., Jr., S.J. "Convergence of Flannery O'Connor and Chardin," *Renascence*, XIX (Winter 1967), 41-47, 52.

CAPOTE, Truman. *In Cold Blood* (New York, 1967).

CASH, W. J. *The Mind of the South* (New York, 1941).

CHENEY, Brainard. "Miss O'Connor Creates Unusual Humor Out of Ordinary Sin," *Sewanee Review*, LXXI (Autumn 1963), 644-652.

COLEMAN, Richard. "Flannery O'Connor: A Scrutiny of Two Forms of Her Many-Leveled Art," *Phoenix*, No. 1 (Fall 1967), 30-66.

DAVIS, Barnabas. "Flannery O'Connor: Christian Belief in Recent Fiction," *Listening* (Autumn 1963), 644-652.

DAVIS, David Brion. *Homicide in American Fiction, 1798-1860* (Ithaca, 1957).

DETWEILER, Robert. "The Curse of Christ in Flannery O'Connor's Fiction." *Comparative Literature Studies*, III, No. 2 (1966), 235-245.

DOWELL, Bob. "The Moment of Grace in the Fiction of Flannery O'Connor," *College English*, XXVII (December 1965), 235-239.

DRAKE, Robert. "The Bleeding, Stinking, Mad Shadow of Jesus in the Fiction of Flannery O'Connor," *Comparative Literature Studies*, III, No. 2 (1966).

———. "Hair-Curling Gospel," *The Christian Century*, LXXXII (May 19, 1965), 656.

———. "The Harrowing Evangel of Flannery O'Connor," *The Christian Century*, LXXXI (September 30, 1964), 1200-1202.

———. "Miss O'Connor and the Scandal of Redemption," *Modern Age*, IV (Fall 1960), 428-430.

DUHAMEL, P. Albert. "Flannery O'Connor's Violent View of Reality," *The Catholic World*, CXC (February 1960), 280-285.

DUPEE, F. W. "On Beerbohm's Zuleika," *New York Review of Books*, Vol. VI, No. 10 (June 9, 1966).

Esprit, VII (Winter 1964). A memorial issue for Flannery O'Connor.

Esquire. "The Structure of the American Literary Establishment," July 1963.

FARNHAM, James F. "The Grotesque in Flannery O'Connor," *America*, CV (May 13, 1961), 277, 280-281.

FAULKNER, William. *Sartoris* (New York, 1956).

———. *Light in August* (New York, 1932).

FERRIS, Sumner J. "The Outside and the Inside: Flannery O'Connor's *The Violent Bear It Away*," *Critique*, III (Winter-Spring 1960), 11-19.

FITZGERALD, Robert. "The Countryside and the True Country," *Sewanee Review*, LXX (Summer 1962), 380-394.

————. "Introduction" in Flannery O'Connor, *Everything That Rises Must Converge* (New York, 1965), vii-xxxiv.

FITZGERALD, Sally and Robert. *Flannery O'Connor, Mystery and Manners* (New York, 1969).

FRIEDMAN, Melvin J., and Lewis A. LAWSON, eds. *The Added Dimension: The Art and Mind of Flannery O'Connor* (New York, 1966).

FRIEDMAN, Melvin J. "Flannery O'Connor: Another Legend in Southern Fiction," in Joseph Waldmeir, ed., *Recent American Fiction: Some Critical Views* (Boston, 1963), 231-245.

FROHOCK, W. M. *The Novel of Violence in America, 1920-1950,* (Dallas, 1950).

GABLE, Sister Mariella, O.S.B. "Ecumenic Core in Flannery O'Connor's Fiction," *The American Benedictine Review,* XV (June 1964), 127-143.

GORDON, Caroline. "Flannery O'Connor's *Wise Blood,*" *Critique,* II (Fall 1958), 3-10.

GOSSETT, Louise Y. *Violence in Recent Southern Fiction* (Durham, 1965).

HART, Jane. "Strange Earth, The Stories of Flannery O'Connor," *Georgia Review,* XII (Summer 1958), 215-222.

HAWKES, John. "Flannery O'Connor's Devil," *Sewanee Review,* LXX (Summer 1962), 395-407.

HICKS, Granville. "A Cold Hard Look At Humankind," *Saturday Review,* XLVIII (May 29, 1965), 23-24.

————. "A Writer at Home with Her Heritage," *Saturday Review,* XLV (May 12, 1962), 22-24.

HOWE, Irving. "On Flannery O'Connor," *New York Review of Books,* Vol. V, No. 4 (September 30, 1965).

HYMAN, Stanley Edgar. "Flannery O'Connor's Tattooed Christ," *New Leader,* No. 48 (May 10, 1965), 9-10.

————. *Flannery O'Connor,* University of Minnesota Pamphlets on American Writers, No. 54 (Minneapolis, 1966).

JACOBSON, Josephine. "A Catholic Quartet," *The Christian Scholar,* XLVII (Summer 1964), 139-154.

JEREMY, Sister, C.S.J. *"The Violent Bear It Away:* A Linguistic Education," *Renascence,* XVII (Spring 1964), 11-16.

JONES, Bartlett C. "Depth Psychology and Literary Study," *Midcontinent American Studies Journal,* V, ii (1964), 50-56.

JOSELYN, Sister M. "Thematic Centers in 'The Displaced Person,' " *Studies in Short Fiction,* I, No. 2 (Winter 1964), 85-92.

KANE, Patricia. Review of *Everything That Rises Must Converge, Critique,* VIII, No. 1 (Fall 1965), 85-89.

KANN, Sister Jean Marie, O.S.F. "On 'Everything That Rises Must Converge,' " *Thought,* CCIV (Spring 1967), 154-159.

LAWSON, Lewis A. "Flannery O'Connor and the Grotesque: Wise Blood," *Renascence,* XVIII (Winter 1965), 137-147, 156.

LE CLÉZIO, J. M. G. "L'univers de Flannery O'Connor," *Nouvelle Revue Française* (September 1964), 488-493.

MCCARTHY, John F. "Human Intelligence v. Divine Truth: The Intellectual in Flannery O'Connor's Works," *English Journal,* LV (September 1967), 1143-1148.

MCCOWN, Robert, S. J. "Flannery O'Connor and the Reality of Sin," *The Catholic World,* CLXXXVIII (January 1959), 285-291.

MARKS, W. S. III. "Advertisements for Grace: Flannery O'Connor's A Good Man Is Hard to Find," *Studies in Short Fiction,* IV (Spring 1967), 19-27.

MARX, Leo. *The Machine in the Garden* (New York, 1964).

MEADERS, Margaret Inman. "Flannery O'Connor: Literary Witch," *Colorado Quarterly,* X (Spring 1962), 377-386.

MERTON, Thomas. "The Other Side of Despair," *Critic,* XXIII (October-November 1965), 13-23.

MEYERS, Sister Bertrande, D.C. "Four Stories of Flannery O'Connor," *Thought,* No. 37 (Autumn 1962), 410-426.

NOLDE, Sister M. Simon, O.S.B. *"The Violent Bear It Away:* A Study in Imagery," *Xavier University Studies* (Spring 1962), 180-194.

O'CONNOR, Flannery. *A Good Man Is Hard to Find* (New York, 1955).

——. *Everything That Rises Must Converge* (New York, 1965).

——. *The Violent Bear It Away* (New York, 1960).

——. *Wise Blood* (New York, 1952).

——. "The Geranium," *Accent*, VI (Summer 1946), 245-253.

——. "The Capture," *Mademoiselle* (November 1948), pp. 148-149, 195-196.

——. "The Partridge Festival," *The Critic*, XIII (February-March 1961), 20-23, 82-85.

——. "Why Do the Heathens Rage?" *Esquire*, LX (July 1963), 60-61.

——. "The Church and the Fiction Writer," *America*, SCVI (March 30, 1957), 733-735.

——. "The Fiction Writer and His Country" in Granville Hicks, ed., *The Living Novel: A Symposium* (New York, 1957), 157-164.

——. "Introduction" in Anon., *A Memoir of Mary Ann* (New York, 1961), 3-21.

——. "Living With a Peacock," *Holiday*, XXX (September 1961), 52-53, 110-114.

——. "Some Aspects of the Grotesque in Southern Literature," East Texas State University Lecture (Fall 1962).

QUINN, Sister M. Bernetta, O.S.F. "View From A Rock: The Fiction of Flannery O'Connor and J. F. Powers," *Critique*, Vol. 2, No. 2 (Fall 1958), 20-35.

RECHNITZ, Robert M. "Passionate Pilgrim: Flannery O'Connor's *Wise Blood*," *Georgia Review*, XIX (Summer 1965), 310-316.

ROBBE-GRILLET, Alain. *For A New Novel* (New York, 1965).

RUBIN, Louis D., Jr. "Flannery O'Connor: A Note on Literary Fashion," *Critique*, Vol. 2, No. 2 (Fall 1958).

RUPP, Richard H. "Flannery O'Connor," *The Commonweal*, LXXIX (December 6, 1963), 304-307.

SHERRY, Gerard E. "An Interview with Flannery O'Connor," *The Critic*, XXI (June-July 1963), 29-31.

SMITH, J. Oates. "Ritual and Violence in Flannery O'Connor," *Thought*, XLI (Spring 1960), 545-560.

SNOW, Ollye Tine. "The Functional Gothic Flannery O'Connor," *Southwest Review* (1965), 286-299.

SPIVEY, Ted R. "Flannery O'Connor's View of God and Man," *Studies in Short Fiction*, I (Spring 1964), 200-206.

STELZMANN, Rainulf. "Shock and Orthodoxy: An Interpretation of Flannery O'Connor's Novels and Short Stories," *Xavier University Studies*, II (March 1963), 4-21.

STERN, Richard. "Flannery O'Connor: A Remembrance and Some Letters," *Shenandoah* (Winter 1965), 22-41.

STYRON, William. *The Confessions of Nat Turner* (New York, 1967).

SULLIVAN, Walter. "Flannery O'Connor, Sin and Grace: *Everything That Rises Must Converge*," *The Hollins Critic*, II (September 1965).

The Times Literary Supplement. "Memento Mori," March 24, 1967, 242; April 28, 1967, 372.

The *Union-Recorder*, Milledgeville, Georgia. Vol. CXLIII, No. 48, August 6, 1964.

WALSH, Thomas F. "The Devils of Hawthorne and Flannery O'Connor," *Xavier University Studies*, V (1967), 117-122.

WEDGE, George F. "Two Bibliographers: Flannery O'Connor, J. F. Powers," *Critique: Studies in Modern Fiction*, II (Fall 1958), 59-63.

WOODWARD, C. Vann. *The Burden of Southern History* (New York, 1960).

Notes

CHAPTER I

1. Richard Stern, "Flannery O'Connor: A Remembrance and some Letters," in *Shenandoah*, Vol. XVI, No. 2 (Winter 1965), 5-6.

2. Flannery O'Connor, *Mystery and Manners*, ed. by Sally and Robert Fitzgerald (New York, 1969), 15.

3. Flannery O'Connor, "The Fiction Writer and His Country," in *The Living Novel*, ed. Granville Hicks (New York, 1957), 157.

4. Sister Bertrande Meyers, "Four Stories of Flannery O'Connor," *Thought*, XXXVII (Autumn 1962), 411.

5. Bob Dowell, "The Moment of Grace in the Fiction of Flannery O'Connor," *College English*, XXVII (December 1965), 238.

6. Albert Griffith, "Flannery O'Connor's Salvation Road," *Studies in Short Fiction*, III, No. 3 (Spring 1966), 330.

7. Sister M. Bernetta Quinn, "View From A Rock: The Fiction of Flannery O'Connor and J. F. Powers," *Critique*, Vol. 2, No. 2 (Fall 1958), 24.

8. Sister Mariella Gable, "Ecumenic Core in Flannery O'Connor's Fiction," *The American Benedictine Review*, XV (June 1964), 127.

9. Robert Drake, *Flannery O'Connor*, Contemporary Writers in Christian Perspective Series (Grand Rapids, 1966), 15.

10. Irving Howe, "On Flannery O'Connor," the *New York Review of Books*, Vol. V, No. 4 (Sept. 30, 1965), 16.

11. J. M. G. Le Clézio, "L'univers de Flannery O'Connor," *Nouvelle Revue Francaise*, XIII (September 1964), 491.

12. John Hawkes, "Flannery O'Connor's Devil," *Sewanee Review*, LXX (1962), 398.

13. For a fuller description of the symbolist novel see Virginia Woolf's "Modern Fiction" in *The Common Reader* (London, 1925) and William York Tindall's *The Literary Symbol* (Bloomington, Ind., 1962).

14. Alain Robbe-Grillet, "A Future for the Novel," in *For a New Novel* (New York, 1965), 19.

15. For a fuller account of the New Novel see the essays in *For a New Novel*, and, in addition, Roland Barthes' "Objective Literature, Alain Robbe-Grillet," in *Two Novels by Robbe-Grillet* (New York, 1965), and Susan Sontag's "Nathalie Sarraute and the Novel," and "Godard's *Vivre sa vie*" in *Against Interpretation* (New York, 1969).

16. F. W. Dupee, "On Beerbohm's Zuleika," the *New York Review of Books*, VI, No. 10 (June 9, 1966), 16.

17. In *A Good Man Is Hard to Find*, they are most often like Mrs. Hopewell ("Good Country People"), Mrs. Cope ("A Circle in the Fire"), Susan and Joanne ("A Temple of the Holy Ghost"), Mrs. McIntyre ("The Displaced Person"), Ruby ("A Stroke of Good Fortune"), or their more manipulative counterparts, Mrs. Connin ("The River"), Sally Poker Sash ("A Late Encounter with the Enemy"), and Mrs. Crater ("The Life You Save May Be Your Own"). In *Everything That Rises Must Converge*, they are like Mrs. Chestny ("Everything That Rises Must Converge"), Mrs. May ("Greenleaf"), Mr. Fortune ("A View of the Woods"), Mrs. Fox ("The Enduring Chill"), Thomas's unnamed mother ("The Comforts of Home"), Mr. Sheppard ("The Lame Shall Enter First"), Mrs. Turpin ("Revelation"), and Mr. Parker ("Parker's Back"). All find themselves in conflict with incarnations of the past. For example, Mrs. Hopewell contends with her daughter, Mrs. Cope with three boys, Susan and

Joanne are abused by their cousin, Mrs. Connin struggles with the preacher, Mrs. Crater is defeated by Shiftlet, Ruby by her pregnancy, Sally Poker Sash by death, and Mrs. McIntyre by Mrs. Shortley. In *Everything That Rises Must Converge*, the conflict is usually between parent and child: Mrs. Chestny is rebuked by her son, Mrs. May by her sons and the Greenleaf boys, Mr. Fortune by his grand-daughter Mary Fortune Pitts, Mrs. Fox by her son Asbury; Thomas's mother is killed by her son, Mr. Sheppard hurt by Johnson, Mr. Parker by his wife, and Mrs. Turpin falls prey to a Wellesley girl, daughter of her social "double."

18. Graham Greene, *A Burnt-Out Case* (New York, 1961), 33.

CHAPTER 2

1. For a religious interpretation see Robert Drake, *Flannery O'Connor*, Contemporary Writers in Christian Perspective Series (Grand Rapids, 1966) Drake sees Taulkinham as a modern Sodom where the Christian ascetic, Haze, sees different attitudes toward the Christian religion.

2. For a religious interpretation see Jonathan Baumbach, "The Acid of God's Grace: The Fiction of Flannery O'Connor," *Georgia Review*, XVII (Fall 1963), 335. Baumbach sees Haze as a symbol of mystical religion and Enoch as one of organized religion.

3. Stanley Edgar Hyman, *Flannery O'Connor*, University of Minnesota Pamphlets on American Writers, No. 54 (Minneapolis, 1966), 14-15. Hyman thinks *Wise Blood* charts Motes's progress toward Bethlehem from original sin, through an affirmation of faith by blasphemy, to a sense of vocation culminating in his ordination.

4. For a religious interpretation see Hyman, p. 13. Hyman thinks Motes's attitude signifies the *noli me tangere* of the risen Christ in the Gospel of St. Luke.

5. For a religious interpretation see Caroline Gordon, "Flannery O'Connor's *Wise Blood*," *Critique*, Vol. 2, No. 2 (Fall 1958), 76. Gordon sees the world of the novel as simply a world without Christ. Motes, to her, is a Jesus *malgré lui* in a world that has rejected the Redemption.

6. For a religious interpretation see Lewis A. Lawson, "Flannery O'Connor and the Grotesque: *Wise Blood*," *Renascence* XVIII (Spring 1965), 156. Lawson sees Motes as an exemplar of Old Testament guilt and his suffering as an attempt at expiation.

7. For a religious interpretation see Sumner J. Ferris, "The Outside and the Inside: Flannery O'Connor's *The Violent Bear It Away*," *Critique*, III, ii (Winter-Spring 1960), 15. Ferris explains the novel in relation to the exegesis on its title —taken from Matthew 11:12 in Douai—in *A Catholic Commentary on the Holy Scriptures*. The commentary says, "With Christ's ministry begun, the faithful may reach the kingdom of Heaven," and, conversely, "Pharisees, despite John's prophecy and Christ's ministry, still do not believe and try to deny the faithful their reward."

8. For a religious interpretation see Brainard Cheney, "Miss O'Connor Creates Unusual Humor Out of Ordinary Sin," *Sewanee Review*, LXXI (Autumn 1963), 645. Cheney hears this voice as the devil's.

9. For a religious interpretation see Drake, p. 34, who sees Rayber as Lucifer and the homosexual as another manifestation of the devil.

10. For a religious interpretation see Sister Jeremy, "*The Violent Bear It Away*: A Linguistic Education," *Renascence*, XVII (Spring 1964), 11. Jeremy discusses the pattern of the novel as the transmission of an oral, biblical tradition to a sceptical disciple.

11. For a religious interpretation see Hyman, p. 23. Hyman says "the sodomic rape . . . is at once the ultimate violation of the untouchable anointed of the Lord, a naturalistic explanation for the shaman's spirit possession, and a shocking and effective metaphor for seizure by divine purpose."

12. For a different religious interpretation see Albert P. Duhamel, "Flannery O'Connor's Violent View of Reality," *The Catholic World,* CXC (February 1960), 282. Duhamel sees young Tarwater as a "latter day Huck Finn," a typical boy in the process of discovering his vocation.

CHAPTER 3

1. For a religious interpretation see Albert Griffith, "Flannery O'Connor's Salvation Road," *Studies in Short Fiction,* III, No. 3 (Spring 1966) p. 330. Griffith sees Shiftlet as a Jesus preaching the Christian doctrine of dichotomy.

2. For a religious interpretation see Robert Drake, *Flannery O'Connor,* Contemporary Writers in Christian Perspective Series (Grand Rapids, 1966), 25. Drake sees Pointer as an anti-Christ, a devil who "wins something of our admiration: he may be a devil but he's not, as is Hulga, a fool."

3. For a standard religious interpretation, see Maurice Bassan, "Flannery O'Connor's Way: Shock with Moral Intent," *Renascence,* XV (Summer 1963), 211. Bassan thinks the child has a saintly honesty that pierces all shams and interprets the story as an image of grace as conceived by a beautifully disciplined Catholic mind.

4. Although there is no official church translation of the "*Tantum Ergo,*" there seem to be only minor differences among the translations I have been able to locate. For example, the hymn appears on the hymn cards of the Church of St. Jean the Baptist and the Church of St. Vincent Ferrer, both in Manhattan, as:

> Down in adoration falling
> Lo, the sacred Host we hail;
> Lo, o'er ancient forms departing
> Newer rites of grace prevail;
> Faith for all defects supplying
> Where the feeble senses fail.

To the everlasting Father
And the Son who reigns on high
With the Holy Ghost proceeding
Forth from each eternally
Be salvation, honor, blessing,
Might and endless majesty.

In the *St. Andrew Daily Missal* the second stanza is translated exactly like the one quoted above but the first appears as:

Lowly bending, deep adoring
Lo! The Sacrament we hail.
Types and shadows have their ending
Newer rites of grace prevail;
Faith for all defects supplying
Where the feeble senses fail.

The literal translation that appears in the text is my own.

CHAPTER 4

1. For a religious interpretation, see Walter Sullivan, "Flannery O'Connor, Sin and Grace: *Everything That Rises Must Converge*," *Hollins Critic*, II (September 1965), 7. Sullivan sees the blood and heart diseases that flourish in the collection simply as examples of the burden of being human, of the weakness of the human body before God. The conflicts of "intellectuals" like Julian and Wesley he thinks demonstrate the need for salvation and the inefficacy of reason to reach it.

2. For a religious interpretation see Robert Drake, *Flannery O'Connor*, Contemporary Writers in Christian Perspective Series (Grand Rapids, 1966), 30. Drake feels both Julian and Asbury suffer from pride of intellect.

3. For a more favorable look at the priesthood, see Robert Fitzgerald, "The Countryside and the True Country," *Sewa-*

nee Review, LXX (Summer, 1962), 380. The priest alone in "The Displaced Person" can see the peacock—which Fitzgerald sees as a symbol of Christian plenitude—because he is the representative of the universal church.

4. For a religious interpretation see Drake, p. 28. Drake sees Mrs. May's death on the bull's horns as an image of judgment and damnation.

5. For a religious interpretation see Sister Bertrande Meyers, "Four Stories of Flannery O'Connor," *Thought*, XXVII (Autumn 1962), 411. Sister Bertrande sees the action of "The Comforts of Home" as a demonstration of the power of redemptive grace.

6. For a religious interpretation see Drake, p. 31. Drake sees Mrs. Turpin's vision as a dramatization of the Christian paradox: the first shall be last and the last first. He thinks her vision signifies that she is on the road to salvation.

For an opposite religious interpretation see Stanley Edgar Hyman, *Flannery O'Connor*, University of Minnesota Pamphlets on American Writers, No. 54 (Minneapolis, 1966), 36. Hyman thinks Mrs. Turpin is going to hell.

7. In his fine review of *Everything That Rises Must Converge*, Irving Howe points out that Mrs. Turpin's vision of heaven is a vision of total chaos.

CHAPTER 5

1. William Faulkner, *Sartoris* (New York, 1956), 9.

2. William Faulkner, *Light in August* (New York, 1932), 439-440.

3. William Styron, *The Confessions of Nat Turner* (New York, 1967), 413-415.

4. Truman Capote, *In Cold Blood* (New York, 1967), 243-245.

5. *Light in August*, p. 424.

6. *Confessions of Nat Turner*, p. 370.

7. Ibid., p. 372.

8. For a religious interpretation see Ted R. Spivey, "Flannery O'Connor's View of God and Man," *Studies in Short Fiction*, I (Spring 1964), 203. Spivey sees the Misfit's act as an evil resulting from the absence of Christ and the rejection of redemptive love as represented by the grandmother. *See also* Sister M. Martin, "O'Connor's *A Good Man Is Hard To Find*," *Explicator*, XXIV (Spring 1965), Item 19. Sister Martin feels the story is about goodness and thinks it suggests a real standard of goodness as unity before God.

Index